LIVING
OUR NEW LIFE
IN CHRIST

A WESLEYAN SPIRITUALITY FOR TODAY

JERRY L. MERCER

DISCIPLESHIP RESOURCES

P.O. BOX 340003 • NASHVILLE, TN 37203-0003
www.discipleshipresources.org

Dedication
This book is dedicated to my daughters
(Donnel, Deborah, Kathryn, Diane),
four shining lights in my eastern sky.

Cover design by Sharon Anderson

Book design by Joey McNair

ISBN 0-88177-275-5

Library of Congress Catalog Card No. 98-88822

DR275

Contents

Special Mention

I want to make special mention of several people who brought this book to completion:

- Dr. Henk Pieterse, former acquisitions editor for Discipleship Resources, had confidence that I could write on a subject close to his heart. Thanks for trusting me with this assignment.
- The Reverend John P. "Jack" Gilbert, an editor with whom I have worked in the past, encouraged me with his fine work and words.
- Heidi Hewitt, assistant editor for Discipleship Resources, kept me straight on the details.
- My wife, Ruth, lives with me and my historical "friends" (such as the Wesley brothers) without complaining.
- The Reverend B. G. Williams, my brother-in-law, whose love for Wesley was a reminder to me of our church's glorious (and sometimes ragged) past.
- Asbury Theological Seminary, my former school, provided me with a sabbatical for work on this project.
- Others who assisted me in this work, unknown to me but known to God. I thank you.

The Call and the Craving

*T*he Christian faith is like an ocean: beautiful and immense, beckoning and mysterious.

For several years my wife, Ruth, and I vacationed on the south beach of Hilton Head Island. Daily we would walk along the beach, listening to the gentle roll of the ocean waves. One morning we saw a group of children playing in a large tide pool that had been created by the retreating waters. In it were trapped many little fish. We watched for a while as the children splashed and laughed and chased the fish. The children were happy, totally absorbed in the warm and friendly water, which was as much as a foot deep in places. It must have seemed quite deep to the children. Behind them the crest of the mighty ocean rose and sank, like a giant breathing, as far as the eye could see. The sun created acres of diamonds on its surface waves. But the children never seemed to notice.

Ruth and I were watching a parable. Like those little children, many of us worship a God of the tide pool, never quite realizing that just beyond us is the beginning of the depths, and never quite hearing the rhythmic invitation of the ocean to come, to explore, to sing its song.

This book is for those who have looked up and seen the ocean of God's love, for those who want to plunge into the very depths of that love, for those who must now leave the tide pool and venture forth in faith into the deep waters of God's call upon their lives. John and Charles

Wesley, leaders of "the people called Methodists,"[1] understood this desire. In their lives they, too, had moved from the tide pool to the ocean of God's love. For them this meant hearing the call to a life dedicated to the Christian teaching: "Whatever you do, in word or deed, do everything in the name of the Lord Jesus, giving thanks to God the Father through him" (Colossians 3:17). It meant for them, and it means for us, moving beyond the shallows to the great deep of the Spirit.

This is not a one-time act, such as joining a church or a fraternity. The call to the depths is a call to a particular way of living, and the benefits of this life are what everyone, religious or not, wants. As human beings, we need to know that our lives count, that we are free to express ourselves, that a great love is really possible, and that God is just over the horizon ahead of us. These deep needs are mere unmet frustrations to many people, but the Wesleys saw them as opportunities for a relationship that changes frustrations into fulfillment. They saw clearly that our problems are more with our heart than with our head. And seeing the problem, they saw the answer: The answer is love; the way is faith; the result is happiness. This is the way of truth, the way of Jesus of Nazareth, our common Lord.

And what is this way? It is the way of an upright and responsible life before God. It is actually our response to the gospel. "Like obedient children," the apostle Peter writes, "do not be conformed to the desires that you formerly had in ignorance. Instead, as he who called you is holy, be holy yourselves in all your conduct; for it is written, 'You shall be holy, for I [the Lord] am holy'" (1 Peter 1:14-16). As much as it may strain our concepts of who we are and what we are, we are called to be God's holy people.

That kind of language was perfectly understandable in the first century. Today, such language may sound strange, even remote. If Peter had written that we should be just and good, people after God's own will, we would understand that; then the language of the New Testament would be obvious to us. We would see that Peter wants us to be upright in morality and responsible in our relationships, in the fullest sense of those words. To the Wesleys this meant that we draw our identity from God and see our lives as extensions of God's will. And this begins to happen when Jesus Christ makes us new people and puts us on the path to uprightness in life—that is, to what the Wesley brothers would call holiness of heart. When we hear Jesus' call to go beyond mediocrity, we have heard the call to take seriously the demand that, believe it or not, we are to be as Christ is in this world.

Our New Life in Christ

Jesus Christ is not just some figure from the distant past, a man whose life and death played prominently in the evolution of culture. Rather, Christ has shown himself to be a living presence in our lives, one who opened and continues to open the kingdom of God to us. Christ moves upon us as a force, as powerful and as inexorable as the tide that filled the pools on that beach. Though the church writes creeds about Christ, he is more than any creed. Christ is more than any book that has been written about him. Jesus the Christ is, as the writers of the New Testament express, the Son of God come into the world to carry out the plan of God for the restoration of the world. Jesus Christ is bringing the world to God, as the apostle Paul says. Those of us who follow Christ Jesus are energized by grace to live for him in every possible way. To be a Christian is to grow in Christ's likeness, to have Christ's mind, to share Christ's suffering love for the world. This is the grace that makes us different. This is, so to speak, "the depths" of God.

The Wesleys, like many other spiritual guides, understood that life in Christ is a call and a craving. Actually, this is true whenever authentic love of any kind breaks into our lives. By its nature, love calls us to share its life; in doing that, love sets up in us a craving for more love. We experience this when we are deeply in love with another person. This is especially true when that other is God. We cannot study the Wesleys for long before realizing that their great emphasis is on the fabulous love of God. In sermons, in letters, in tracts, and in hymns that still illuminate our worship, the Wesleys teach that God reaches out to us in our loneliness and sin, forgives and empowers us, and gracefully leads us on the path of increasing love all the way to the kingdom of love, the kingdom of God. This is a message we want to hear because we naturally want love; we want to be bonded to someone who genuinely cares about us. Sensing this love in our lives, we want to share it with others. Love naturally touches others, and in Christ we want to live out his central teaching: to love God with all that we are and to love others as we love ourselves (Mark 12:29-31). We are called by God to participate in God's love and to share that divine love, a love that alone can change the world.

How do the Wesleys teach us about new life in Christ? They do it through song and sermon. Though both brothers were poets and proclaimers, Charles is known more for his hymnody and John for his preaching and writing. Together they moved Great Britain toward moral and spiritual renewal, and they will move us as well. We will be looking at the sermons of John Wesley.[2] We will also be looking at Charles Wesley's *A Collection of Hymns for the Use of the People Called Methodists.*[3] These works will encourage us, as the baptismal liturgy of The United Methodist Church proclaims, to renounce the works of evil and to take up with our whole heart the new life Christ sets before us. What is this life? It is the life of self-giving love to God and to others. It is a joyous life of struggle with ourselves and with our circumstances. The struggle is joyous because in our pain—as in our pleasure—God comes to us, as Charles Wesley says, as that "love divine" that excels all other loves.[4]

Living Deeply

As you may know, the Wesleys and the early Methodist people were captured by a grand obsession: to live as deeply as possible what it means to be "altogether a Christian,"[5] as John Wesley put it. In his famous tract, *The Character of a Methodist,* John Wesley says Jesus Christ makes his followers happy, hopeful, praying, loving, gentle, sincere, obedient, growing, witnessing, faithful people. This is what Wesley means by being "Methodist." It means wanting to experience as much as possible the fully satisfying life God gives. What Wesley describes is exactly the kind of person we would like to be and the kind of neighbor we would like to have.

John Wesley knew that such a life does not happen with a snap of the fingers. In fact, it may not happen at all. Historians tell us that many people who were converted in the Wesleyan Awakening in England could not keep their confidence in Christ, so they eventually drifted away. This realization troubled both Wesleys because they saw how true Jesus' words are, that the road to the Kingdom is narrow and not many stay on that road to its final destination. One of the most difficult things I faced as a pastor was members who at one time were shining Christians but for whom the light of inspiration had gone out. I have seen the same thing at seminary when a budding minister lost confidence, and hope slipped away. To be lived successfully, the Christian life requires a kind of doggedness, a stubborn perseverance, a standing firm—what John Wesley described as clinging to Christ.

Wesley was sure that even faithful Christians vary widely in their desire to live for Christ. Not all have the same determination. The New Testament teaches this. There are babes in Christ, just as there are soldiers in Christ. Wesley wanted all of us to move on to maturity, to grow out of babyhood and become spiritual adults. Wesley knew that to do this we must be loyal to God and seek God. I am sure you know people who are examples of mature Christian faith. In fact, we commit ourselves to serious growth when we promise to God at our baptism that we will be true to our commitment no matter what.

One of the misleading things about a book this size is that it may give some people the idea that knowledge of God can be quickly gained and that the life of Christ in us can be easily lived. Nothing could be further from the truth. As we will see, the knowledge of God requires trust and patience; growth in Christ requires determination, prayer, and steadiness in the face of temptation, unexpected and unasked-for evil, and ambiguity. Holiness is not cheap.

The goals of Christian experience, for the Wesleys, are twofold: The first goal is to know God as fully as possible; the second is to experience eternal life in God's kingdom of glory. These goals are related, since faithful living now leads to eternal life with God later. These goals are not private, but are lived out on our jobs, among our friends, and in the way we interact with people who are problems for us. These goals are not accomplished by doing good alone; salvation is not a reward for effort, but is instead a gift from God. The goals of Christian experience and the means to reach those goals are without question the free gift of God in Christ by the Holy Spirit. No one can say to God, "I earned your love." Instead, we hope to hear, "Come, you that are blessed by my Father, inherit the kingdom prepared for you from the foundation of the world" (Matthew 25:34). Christ invites; we accept. Christ empowers; we rejoice. Christ gives; we share.

John and Charles Wesley were powerfully moved by our Lord's statement on love in what we call the Sermon on the Mount: "Be perfect, therefore, as your heavenly Father is perfect" (Matthew 5:48). Jesus speaks here about love as wanting and working for the best for others, even our enemies. This is a high mark, one that may look impossible at times. Such a life was not easy even for Jesus; yet he demonstrated this kind of love throughout his life, especially during his trial and while on the cross. The Wesleys believed that our lives can be so filled with God that selfless concern can be shown to all, even to those who exploit us. (This level of love, as we will see, is not a substitute for justice or righteousness; rather, it is the foundation for both.) The quest for this sense of love permeates the songs and sermons of the first Methodists. This is the kind of love the early Methodists tried to demonstrate in the way they treated other people. The point, according to the Wesleys, is that Jesus wants us to be as he is in our thoughts and actions. The Wesleys believed that this love is a possibility for us now as we make our way to the Kingdom. To even think about such magnificent love in our lives is exciting.

A Remarkable Journey

We may fall in love quite spontaneously, but there is an order to the experience of love in our salvation. You see, God normally works with us in certain ways. This book will unfold the Wesley brothers' understanding of how God works in our lives to make us fully formed Christians, and it will explain what that means. The chapters lead us from our first steps in faith to their culmination in the kingdom of God.

- The opening chapter describes the first step, our conversion to Christ. This is the very beginning of upright or holy living.
- The second chapter deals with the problem of evil, especially in our world, that threatens our relationship with Christ and causes stress in our lives.
- The third chapter addresses how we grow in consecration to God as people of faith. This is the personal side of spirituality.
- The fourth chapter shows how our walk with God relates to the needs of other people in our lives. This is the social side of spirituality.
- The fifth chapter, the heart of the book, is concerned with the Wesleyan teaching on ever-increasing love as the constant goal of Christian faith.
- The sixth chapter explores the importance of the Wesleys' teaching for our life in the larger church.
- The final chapter shows the reality of assuring grace and the Wesleys' conviction that the Christian experience of holiness and happiness is "heaven below,"[6] leading to heaven above.

Since you are *in Christ,* you are on a remarkable journey. It is a journey that will revolutionize your life for the better. As you have discovered already, there is power in the good news of God's love alive in Christ. John and Charles Wesley believed that this faith in God's power can liberate us from the downward pull of sin and fear and fill us with the marvelous love of God. What does this mean? Certainly this will mean different things to different people. We may discover new levels of understanding in spiritual life, deeper love for God and for other people, a renewed prayer life, increased strength to overcome sin, ability to deal with temptations, and even the courage to face death with hope. It may sensitize us to the needs of suffering people and perhaps energize us to try to do something about their plight. Upright or holy living touches every aspect of our lives and enhances life to the fullest. The grace of God de-compartmentalizes our lives.

But here I must be perfectly clear. The irony is that these and other benefits come to us not because we seek them but because we seek God. We look for the One who loves us, knowing that

God will put in our lives just those strengths and attitudes we need to serve God and others. We may not know exactly what we need, but God does. To trust in God is to say to God, "Whatever you want for me is what I want." Because true love is totally self-giving, we know that God will love us in the way we need most and in the way that will give us the greatest sense of fulfillment and peace. We want what God wants for us. We do not tell God what is best for us; we listen to God so that we can learn what is best for us. So let us be settled on one thing as we begin our study: We want God. We will listen to God. We will trust God.

Therefore, I invite you to walk with me through the spiritual teachings of John and Charles Wesley on the fullness of God's love alive in your heart. Learn from them and pray about what you learn. As you turn to Chapter 1, open your mind and heart to God. This will be for you a journey of discovery and joy. It will be a journey to the depths.

ENDNOTES

1 From "A Plain Account of the People Called Methodists," in *The Works of John Wesley,* Volume VIII (Grand Rapids: Zondervan Publishing House, 1872 reprint), page 248.

2 "Sermons," in *The Works of John Wesley,* Volumes 1–4, edited by Albert C. Outler (Nashville: Abingdon Press; Volume 1, 1984; Volume 2, 1985; Volume 3, 1986; Volume 4, 1987).

3 "A Collection of Hymns for the Use of the People Called Methodists," in *The Works of John Wesley,* Volume 7, edited by Franz Hildebrandt and Oliver A. Beckerlegge, with the assistance of James Dale (Nashville: Abingdon Press, 1983).

4 From "Love Divine, All Loves Excelling," by Charles Wesley, in *The United Methodist Hymnal* (Nashville: The United Methodist Publishing House, 1989), 384.

5 From "The Almost Christian," in *The Works of John Wesley,* Volume 1, edited by Albert C. Outler, page 131. © 1984 Abingdon Press. Used by permission.

6 From "Describing the Pleasantness of Religion," in *The Works of John Wesley,* Volume 7, edited by Franz Hildebrandt and Oliver A. Beckerlegge, with the assistance of James Dale, page 103. © 1983 Abingdon Press. Used by permission.

Chapter 1

God's New People

*D*o you have a formula for curing the blahs? Psychologists advise us not to go shopping. Many of us would pick out an appealing movie, get some popcorn, and sink into another world for awhile. After all, movies are made to give us a break. When I taught a "Church and Cinema" course, I learned that the first emotional need screenwriters take into account when they produce movie scripts is our need for excitement to offset feelings of boredom or the blues. A good screenplay provides the audience in the dark with new challenges, new experiences—that is, an adventure. Screenwriters know that if they are successful in doing this, we will come.

Still, even Hollywood's best would not have been enough for the most noted pessimist in the Old Testament, the anonymous author of Ecclesiastes. Early in his letter, he grumbles:

> What has been is what will be,
>   and what has been done is what
>   will be done;
>   there is nothing new under the sun.
> Is there a thing of which it is said,
>   "See, this is new"?
> It has already been,
>   in the ages before us.
>   (Ecclesiastes 1:9-10)

The writer had tried it all—sex, power, money—and it was all "vanity of vanities" (1:2). He had had more than enough. But this guy was still bored and thought life was futile. A lot of modern people know how he felt. It is strange but true that people who think peace is tiresome prefer war to peace. Better to be killed off violently than pecked to death by time! At least in war we live on the edge; in war, life seems delicious. I will have to admit, however, that this is not my feeling.

Into this kind of human dread of common life comes the good news, with new words about life and new ways of thinking about time. In the midst of tremendous anxiety and devastation, the prophet Jeremiah boldly announces:

> But this I call to mind,
>   and therefore I have hope:
> The steadfast love of the LORD never ceases,
>   his mercies never come to an end;
> they are new every morning;
>   great is your faithfulness.
> "The LORD is my portion," says my soul,
>   "therefore I will hope in him."
> The LORD is good to those who wait for him,
>   to the soul that seeks him.
>   (Lamentations 3:21-25)

The early church saw in prophecies such as this a hint of what was to happen in the life and ministry of the Messiah. He would bring a "new covenant," establish a "new people," give his followers a "new name," teach a "new commandment," even give us a "new self." No wonder the apostle Paul exclaims: "So if anyone is in Christ, there is a new creation: everything old has passed away; see, everything has become new!" (2 Corinthians 5:17). In the last book of the Bible, the writer could foresee the time when God would create a "new heaven" and a "new earth" (21:1). Whatever else it was, the good news of Jesus Christ was to the people of the first century anything but dull and meaningless. It was a message of newness, freshness. Later, in the Book of Acts, the first Christians— women and men and even youth and children—could not be held back by the threat of the whip or death in the arena as they freely witnessed to all who would hear that Jesus Christ could set people free to love God and to love life and be fulfilled in both, no matter what their circumstances.

This life and hope Jesus brings was not lost on John and Charles Wesley or their followers, either. In this first chapter, we will explore their insights on our new life of grace, our old life of sin, and the importance of baptism. This will prepare us for upcoming chapters dealing with the threat of evil and how we can grow in faith and purity.

Our New First Word

The new first word for Christians is *God*. To say that *God* is our first word is to say that in Christ we have been restored to the ancient rhythms of life itself, that *God* is our first word in terms of importance. For most of recorded history, serious talk about God in the marketplace, in the halls of government, and in family life was not at all strange. Even the fool in Psalm 14:1, who says "There is no God," still believes in a god of some kind. The fool chooses to live as though it makes no difference that God exists. It has been only since the turn of the eighteenth century that some people in Europe began to say that God did not exist, and meant it literally. That continues to be an influential message today. To us who believe, however, God is the foundation of life and of all reality. Christ helps us see this. When we say "God," we say who we are.

John Wesley wrote prayers for each day of the week. In the prayer for Sunday evening, Wesley tells God that he (Wesley) belongs only to God and that he (Wesley) wants only to do what God wills, which means loving God above everything else.[1] At the outset of this prayer of praise and confession, Wesley calls attention to themes on the character of God, themes that show up in his preaching: (1) God cares for us like a good parent cares, (2) God's will can be trusted, and (3) God will guide us in the right way. Let's take a look at each of these themes.

God cares for us like a good parent cares. Without question, the central teaching of the Bible is that God loves us like a good parent loves and provides for our salvation. The most obvious parable of Jesus on this theme is the well-known story of the waiting father in Luke 15:11-32. This father has two ungrateful sons who, according to cultural understanding, wish their father were dead. In the course of the parable, the younger son repents of his bad attitude, but the older son continues to rebel. The repentant son is restored; the destiny of the other son is unknown. The behavior of both is, of course, socially unacceptable, and the father would be expected in that society to kick them out; yet he does not do this. The humble father goes far beyond what is expected, even publicly humiliating himself, in trying to reconcile with his two sons. Jesus' point in the parable would have been obvious to the Pharisees for whom it was told. They would have been offended by this teaching because they could see themselves in the sons, especially in the attitude of the older one. But Jesus wanted them to see the Father, the God of love, who wants all his children safe at home.

This good-parent love of God comes to us as part of God's "strange design," as Charles Wesley calls it, through the cross. The essence of love is that God has come to us in the person and work of Jesus of Nazareth, and that the death of Jesus is the primary demonstration of that grand, divine love.

Charles Wesley speaks of God's restoring love in the second stanza of the hymn "And Can It Be That I Should Gain," which we still sing today:

> 'Tis mystery all: th'Immortal dies!
>> Who can explore his strange design?
> In vain the first-born seraph tries
>> To sound the depths of love divine.
> 'Tis mercy all! Let earth adore;
> Let angel minds inquire no more.[2]

Charles Wesley writes of the all-encompassing "mystery" and "mercy" of the death of Jesus, something even the heavenly beings (angels and seraphim) cannot fathom. What we should do is return love for love, that is, "adore" the One who loves us more deeply (the "depths") than we can know. Here Wesley echoes the apostle Paul: "May I never boast of anything except the cross of our Lord Jesus Christ, by which the world has been crucified to me, and I to the world" (Galatians 6:14). Here it is, the love of God that grabs us and holds us fast. God has sacrificed so that we might live.

God's will can be trusted. On his deathbed, John Wesley looked back over a long life and ministry and told those watching that the best thing of all is that God is "with us." Wesley had learned to interpret God's actions in the world as something good, though not always easy to understand. He had learned to trust God and wanted us to live with that confidence as well. In his Sunday prayer I referred to on page 15, Wesley says that he is glad to be in God's hands. He is content to rest in God because he is sure that what God wants for us is good. This is an important point, because over the years I have met many Christians who were anxious and confused about God's will. This is particularly true when suffering comes and we do not comprehend what part, if any, God's plays in that suffering. Good fortune does not seem to bother us, but pain is another matter.

Why are we tempted to question God when things look bad? Wesley is quick to answer that we do not have enough patience and have not learned to trust God and wait, which is a constant theme in the Psalms. Wesley, who was no stranger to trouble, often found comfort in James 1:2-3: "My brothers and sisters, whenever you face trials of any kind, consider it nothing but joy, because you know that the testing of your faith produces endurance."

According to Wesley, considering our trials as joy means that we have reached the highest level of patience. Did John Wesley know about Francis of Assisi, a thirteenth-century saint who saw God's love in all kinds of trials and counted it all joy to suffer? I cannot verify that Wesley knew about Francis of Assisi, but I think Wesley's words certainly echo Saint Francis.

For us to trust God when things are going badly calls on spiritual resources we might not know we have. Even Elie Wiesel, the haunted Jewish author and Nazi death camp survivor, says our pain is God's pain, even when God is the cause of that pain. God is indeed with us, though we may not be able to see it immediately. Although never in Wiesel's extreme circumstances, Wesley, like Wiesel, urges us to be patient during trials. Such patience is more than passive endurance; it is active waiting for God. When the going is particularly bad, this is particularly true. During those times when our spirits are heavy, we are never left without God. John Wesley urges us not to rush to judgment when we are in trouble: Do not assume God has left you. Who knows, God may be using something unpleasant to strengthen your faith. Trust God; God has your best interests in mind.

God will guide us in the right way. When Wesley prays "Do with me what seems good in your sight,"³ he is praying for God's guidance in all things. Confident of God's good will, Wesley could expect God's guidance in everything. When I attended seminary as a student, we talked a lot about God's omniscience, which simply means that God knows all things. We do not use that kind of technical language much anymore, but we still mean that God knows more than we do and knows what is best for us. Some ministers in Wesley's day did not believe that God guides us in our daily lives. Those ministers did not think God *could not* guide us; they thought God *does not* guide us. "We have the freedom to think and make choices," they said. "Why trouble God about things we can do?" Why? Wesley knew it is because we need God to help us. We cannot see what is ahead of us. Wesley knew what the psalmist knew:

> The LORD is my shepherd, I shall not want.
>   He makes me lie down in green pastures;
> he leads me beside still waters;
>   he restores my soul.
> He leads me in right paths
>   for his name's sake.
>
> (Psalm 23:1-3)

The psalmist affirms that God is with him even in the shadow of death, and that God's "rod" and "staff" comfort him. And well they should, because if God does not guide us through some of life's difficulties, we will not make it on our own. So our new first word as Christians is *God.* We have learned to love God and to trust God. We have learned that God wants the best for us. And that best is love.

Our Old First Word

If as Christians our new first word is *God,* then what was our old first word? It was simply *me.* When we say "God," we also say "grace"; and when we say "me," we also say "sin." Do not mistake the Wesleys here. By *sin* the Wesleys mean something that happens first inside our hearts. This means that *sin* is a powerful word. Even in common talk, the word *sin* stands for something gone wrong. But how can the word *me* be wrong? Because sometimes, maybe most of the time, *me* crowds out God and other people.

A man I know was deeply troubled about his son's bad public behavior—it was criminal behavior. The father's reactions were clear. He reacted strongly to his son's sins not because of what they were doing to his son but because of how he thought those sins reflected on him, the father. In this instance, *me* crowded out *son*, and the father was therefore sinning against the son. *Me* can mean "my rights, forget about yours; my agenda, forget about yours; my pleasure, forget about yours."

The Wesleys use the word *inbred* to express the source of this *me* sin. *Inbred* means that at the core of my being, I value *me* more than anything else. This *me* is powerful. One psychologist uses the word *willfulness* to describe this *me,* which means that I will shape life to suit my fancy. But what I really need to be fulfilled personally and to be a responsible member of the community is to be willing—that is, willing to learn, willing to help, willing to acknowledge God. To be changed from *me* to *God,* from *willfulness* to *willing-ness,* changes all of the values of my life. How does this change happen? The Wesleys tell us:

The first step is repentance. No one likes to be told she or he has done wrong. Every teacher, social worker, and corrections officer knows the resistance that comes when people think they are being challenged or told what to do. This is one reason so many people have trouble with authority figures. We tend to see such people as judges over our lives, which is uncomfortable. Who among us likes to see a shaking index finger pointed at her or him? Yet the message of the gospel is that we have done wrong, and that in order to advance in spiritual life, we must come to the place where we admit it, take responsibility for our actions, ask forgiveness, and change our behavior. We can repress that truth or deny it, but most of us know when we have done wrong. In fact, one way psychiatrists know we have a healthy ego is if we have a conscience and can listen to it.

This message of repentance, which is so crucial in understanding the preaching of Jesus and the early church, calls for a fundamental change in our behavior. Defending his ministry before King Agrippa, the apostle Paul says he "declared first to those in Damascus, then in Jerusalem and throughout the countryside of Judea, and also to the Gentiles, that they should repent and turn to God and do deeds consistent with repentance" (Acts 26:20). Such a deep-seated change of heart always involves our response to God and our relationship to others. For example, true repentance changes us from takers to givers. The object of repentance is to restore us to God, so that we might participate in "righteousness and peace and joy in the Holy Spirit" (Romans 14:17). Acts such as truly being sorry for sins, consciously turning from those sins, and beginning to live right can at first seem hard to do, but they have wonderful results in bringing us into the family of God and making us heirs of eternal life.

A section in *A Collection of Hymns for the Use of the People Called Methodists* is called "Praying for Repentance." The first hymn in that section addresses what we are talking about here.[4] In the hymn, Wesley, on behalf of the person seeking repentance and forgiveness, addresses God as "Father of lights," a metaphor that recognizes two things: (1) God shines as light in our darkness; and (2) as a good parent, God wants to forgive us. The good Father, like the good mother, wants to love, to forgive, and to restore. This requires of us a frank, inward searching of our heart. Taking an inward inventory for us, the hymn lists things we need to face. For example, we need to confess that we have been too proud to admit wrong, that we have thought wicked thoughts, that we have not cared about God's will, that we do not like what we see in ourselves, and that we want God to forgive us and lift our burden. That is the down side. The up side is that God hears our confession and pours God's love into our eager hearts.

Repentance is admitting who we really are. As I suggested above, to move from *me* to *God* is radical indeed, especially in a consumer society such as ours, in which we are so used to putting our needs first. Commercials constantly tell us what our needs are and that those needs can be met by designers and manufacturers. I wish it were that simple. The gospel says that what we need is to put God first, and the first step in doing that is to see ourselves as the Lord sees us. In his sermon "The Way to the Kingdom," John Wesley says that repentance involves "self-knowledge." By knowing ourselves, Wesley means

1. that we admit we have been living selfish lives, concerned more with our own good than with the good of others;
2. that we see we have been far from the will of God, choosing to please ourselves instead of being and doing what God says we should;
3. that we have at times wronged others by trying to manipulate them to our own advantage;
4. that we know we deserve God's just anger more than God's mercy and care.

The fourth item seems hard at first. We parents know from our own experience, however, how disappointed, sad, and upset we become when children deliberately disobey family rules. As a child, part of learning from such experiences is seeing that the negative feelings of our parents were appropriate at the time, because our parents loved us and made rules designed to help us. On a much different scale, part of criminal rehabilitation is to see that one's attitudes and behaviors have been destructive and that one really deserves to be punished for hurting someone else. We are taught over and over in Scripture that God is justly angry when people flout God's good will, especially when that leads to injury of others or the denial of their basic rights.

For the Wesleys, the issue was even more serious than what I have suggested so far. In his sermon "Of Hell," John Wesley draws our attention to a subject we would rather not discuss at all. In spite of everything God does for us, Wesley says, some people are so hardened against God that they prefer to live forever without God. I have met only one person in my ministry who told me she was going to hell, knew it, and was satisfied with that. To be honest, I think she was psychologically distressed, though I have no way of knowing for sure. In spite of what I have said about those who love evil, I cannot believe—as the Wesleys could not believe—

that anyone would deliberately choose evil over good. At the same time, the first chapter of Romans and the fiery little book of Jude face the fact that some people are so set against God and so harmful to society that they adamantly refuse to have anything to do with God or good or justice. Such a person cannot possibly know oneself, as Wesley means it.

You may think that the notion of hell is beneath God and that God's redemptive love will eventually take in everyone. I am not trying to justify John Wesley here, but we must grapple with the Hebraic idea that God's holiness is manifested as love and justice. God knows. This is a true mystery. As in all phases of life, we know intuitively that great love means real justice. There are checks and balances. Because life is so precious and happiness so rare yet so universally needed, those who with violence deliberately take both life and happiness away must answer to a human court and to God. Wesley supported a system of law and order in public life for the public good. He also saw in Jesus, the self-giving Savior who appeals to all people everywhere to be reconciled to God, the King of Kings and Lord of Lords. Those who wait before him with faith hear the word of welcome: "Come, you who are blessed by God, enter"; those who have wreaked havoc inherit havoc. Until that time of reckoning, let us all pray and work that all people, including the violent, should bend the knee, with tongues confessing that Jesus Christ is Lord, to the glory of God (Philippians 2:10-11, paraphrased).

Remember Your Baptism

As Christians, our new first word is *God*. To be able to say "God" instead of "me" is freedom indeed. Have you noticed that the more you relate to God, the easier it becomes? It is true that God is always King, but it is also true that in Christ, God becomes a "Friend." The Wesleys believed that we can have an intimate relationship with the Almighty, that we can love—rather than fear—God. When I first began the Christian life, I thought the fact that God knew all about me (my motivations as well as my actions) was an embarrassment. God really knew what was going on with me. Now to think God knows all about me is a relief. God knows—really knows—and loves me still. How wonderful and restful that is.

The church has an important ritual to mark the new life of Christ in us. It is called baptism and is regarded as a sacrament. It is typical for us to celebrate Christian baptism in the morning worship service, so that as many people as possible can participate in it. We practice baptism because of Jesus' commission to his disciples in Matthew 28:19-20a: "Go therefore and make disciples of all nations, baptizing them in the name of the Father and of the Son and of the Holy Spirit, and teaching them to obey everything that I have commanded you." The physical act of baptism is a visible symbol of God's invisible working in our lives. Baptism is a happy moment in the church's life because that act says again that God is at work among us, forgiving our sins and drawing us close.

As an Anglican clergy person, John Wesley taught that baptism is an act of the church that has sacred meaning. Baptism is a sign of a relationship with God. Today we might say baptism is an act that marks the one baptized as a member of the church on earth and the kingdom in heaven. Making promises, applying water that has been blessed, making the sign of the cross on the forehead, and saying prayers of dedication are all important parts of this public turning from wrong and turning to God. During baptism in the early church, new believers wore white clothing, which symbolized their desire to live holy lives before God and others.

As an act, baptism is rooted in the Old Testament ritual of washing as purification. Part of the rite of dedicating Jewish priests for sacred purposes involved such ritual washing. This bathing image is also connected with the Exodus, the deliverance of the Hebrews from Egyptian bondage, in that the people all "passed through the sea" (1 Corinthians 10:1-4). We Christians believe that the Exodus image is a kind of prototype of our relationship with God through Christ. It is a badge of discipleship with deep spiritual meaning. Baptism carries for us images of cleansing, dedication to God, entrance into the body of believers, a marking of discipleship, forgiveness of sins, and a promise of new life to come. Clearly, baptism is for us an important part of Christian community life and witness.

In the early church, candidates for baptism were even given new first names. Baptism is a wonderful ceremony, filled with joy in God.

In his sermon "The Duty of Constant Communion," Wesley tells us that failure to live according to the teachings of the Lord is in effect a renouncing of our baptism. Why would he say that? Well, look at some of the promises we make in the Baptismal Covenant. (The answer to each question is "I do.")

> On behalf of the whole Church, I ask you:
> Do you renounce the spiritual forces of wickedness,
>   reject the evil powers of this world,
>   and repent of your sin?
>
> Do you accept the freedom and power God gives you
>   to resist evil, injustice, and oppression
>   in whatever forms they present themselves?
>
> Do you confess Jesus Christ as your Savior,
> put your whole trust in his grace,
> and promise to serve him as your Lord,
> in union with the Church which Christ has opened
>   to people of all ages, nations, and races?[5]

When infants and children are baptized, we adults are asked if we will nourish these young lives, be examples of true faith before them, and help them lead a Christian life. Baptism is serious to the church.

Occasionally, the church may have an act of "Remembering Your Baptism" as part of its worship service. The minister may read the questions of baptism I mentioned above, with the congregation responding "I do." Then the minister may walk up and down the aisles of the church sprinkling water over the congregation and saying, "Remember your baptism." Being part of such a service is a wonderful experience. Just as couples sometimes repeat their marriage vows, so the church remembers its commitment in order that it may not "[abandon] the love you had at first" for Christ. Such an act recalls the redemptive love of God, the reality of spiritual forces aligned against us, and the need of divine grace to live freely and responsibly. We can feel the electricity of early Methodist zeal for God in the closing part of this prayer to the Trinity at the baptism of an adult:

Father, all thy love reveal!
   Jesus, all thy name impart!
Holy Ghost, renew and dwell
   For ever in [our] heart![6]

Concluding Thoughts

In this chapter, we have seen glimpses of the Wesley brothers' view of a loving God at work among us. We have also seen what this means to us as human beings who have sinned and are seeking forgiveness. We ended the chapter by looking at baptism, the act that combines God's love with our need. This chapter rehearsed the foundation for that life that seeks to live out the fullness of love. As a Christian, you have already experienced something of the deeper meaning of this chapter. From here we move to the combat ahead for us—indeed, the combat in which we live daily. The life of love is not a life of ease. While it produces peace, it often does so in an atmosphere of hostility. But we have the promise of Christ: "And remember, I am with you always, to the end of the age" (Matthew 28:20b). Those who would indeed "go on to perfection"[7] must "[fight] the good fight of faith."[8]

Probing Our Faith

1. Think of a movie or television show you have seen recently. What did that show tell you about the way some people view life? Would those characters have responded to God in any way?

2. What have you learned about God from the teachings of Jesus? How has that affected your life?

3. To whom would you point as the greatest example of God's redeeming grace that you know? What is there about that person that makes you think of God?

4. When you reflect on the questions asked of people being baptized into the church, what new meanings seem to emerge for you?

ENDNOTES

1 See "A Collection of Forms of Prayers," in *The Works of John Wesley*, Volume XI (Grand Rapids: Zondervan Publishing House, 1872 reprint), page 207.

2 From "And Can It Be That I Should Gain," in *The United Methodist Hymnal* (Nashville: The United Methodist Publishing House, 1989), 363. See also "For Believers Rejoicing," in *The Works of John Wesley*, Volume 7, edited by Franz Hildebrandt and Oliver A. Beckerlegge, with the assistance of James Dale (Nashville: Abingdon Press, 1983), page 322.

3 Adapted from "A Collection of Forms of Prayers," in *The Works of John Wesley*, Volume XI (Grand Rapids: Zondervan Publishing House, 1872 reprint), page 207. (The language of the prayer has been rendered in current English.)

4 See "Praying for Repentance," in *The Works of John Wesley*, Volume 7, edited by Franz Hildebrandt and Oliver A. Beckerlegge, with the assistance of James Dale (Nashville: Abingdon Press, 1983), pages 201–2.

5 From "The Baptismal Covenant I," in *The United Methodist Book of Worship*, page 88. © 1976, 1980, 1985, 1989, 1992 The United Methodist Publishing House. Used by permission.

6 From "For Believers Interceding for the World," in *The Works of John Wesley*, Volume 7, edited by Franz Hildebrandt and Oliver A. Beckerlegge, with the assistance of James Dale, page 648. © 1983 Abingdon Press. Used by permission.

7 From "The Repentance of Believers," in *The Works of John Wesley*, Volume 1, edited by Albert C. Outler, page 335. © 1984 Abingdon Press. Used by permission.

8 From "On Sin in Believers," in *The Works of John Wesley*, Volume 1, edited by Albert C. Outler, page 333. © 1984 Abingdon Press. Used by permission.

Chapter 2

Through Fire and Water

*E*very book of the New Testament was written to people who lived under threat. That is a startling fact when we let it really sink in.

To be a Christian in the first century was not easy any way we look at it. We are used to seeing movies about the first Christians being thrown to the lions or tortured in other ways, simply for being Christian. Yet, as long as those images remain on the surface of our minds, we will never really grasp the sense of desperation that characterized the lives of our spiritual ancestors. When we call the gospel "good news," we are saying, as those early Christians said, that when everything else is failing around us, including all our hopes and aspirations, then the mere suggestion that we are loved by God becomes something worth dying for. We Christians today who eat well and sleep between soft sheets in an atmosphere of safety cannot really understand what receiving a letter of encouragement from the apostle Paul meant to persecuted believers of the first century.

In the sixteenth century, a popular book was published by the English historian John Foxe. The book, which was titled simply *Book of Martyrs,* was a frightening chronicle of the horrible way Christians were treated from the first century to his own. Foxe showed that the observations of the writer of Hebrews continued down through the centuries. The author of Hebrews says:

Others were tortured, refusing to accept release, in order to obtain a better resurrection. Others suffered mocking and flogging, and even chains and imprisonment. They were stoned to death, they were sawn in two, they were killed by the sword; they went about in skins of sheep and goats, destitute, persecuted, tormented—of whom the world was not worthy. They wandered in deserts and mountains, and in caves and holes in the ground.

(Hebrews 11:35b-38)

Some of that kind of treatment happens today to Christians around the world. For example, missionaries have recorded real stories of crushing punishment meted out to believers in the Far East and in other parts of the world. If you are interested, surf the Web for tale upon tale of modern martyrs for the cause of Christ.

Our heads spin at such treatment, and even more so at the thought that such persecution actually serves to advance the gospel. "Blood of the martyrs is the seed of the Church," said the early church father Tertullian. It must be seed because Jesus told his disciples they could expect rough handling by the authorities when they witnessed to their belief in God's grace and love. Foxe provides accounts of how that was literally true. The Wesleys, too, experienced harassment during the height of the English Awakening. Early Methodists were often vandalized and brutalized by gangs and bullies. To those early followers of the Wesleys, this was all part of what Jesus meant when he said that his followers must take up their cross and follow him. History teaches us that those who would live upright lives do not have smooth sailing. This is one of the great paradoxes of the quest for goodness.

Wesley saw opposition to the proclamation of the gospel coming from three directions: from spiritual powers, from society at large, and, strangely enough, often from spiritual conflicts in the hearts of Christians. In his letter to the Ephesians, the apostle Paul likens this struggle to a state of war.

This chapter is going to look at the stark spiritual truths that the mere existence of goodness seems to invite reprisal and that experiencing pain is part of growing as a Christian. This chapter will also help prepare us for the next chapter, which deals with spiritual disciplines to help us overcome the threats we face and, in so doing, grow in holiness.

The "Do-Evil"

The Wesley brothers were descended from the English Puritans, who were convinced that the Protestant Reformation of the seventeenth century had not gone far enough in reforming the Church of England. Frustrated, many Puritans left England and Europe for the new world of America, where they hoped to establish the kingdom of God on earth. They believed that this new experiment would result in a pure social order and provide a safe place for Christians to live. From the start, the Puritan experiment was doomed to failure. Today the Puritans are probably most often remembered as the people who held the Salem Witch Trials, in which innocent people were burned at the stake or horribly killed in other ways. The continuing memory of those terrible days makes some of us skittish in believing, as the Puritans did, that a spiritual being who inspires people to do wrong exists. They called the being the Do-Evil (devil) or Satan. To blame a devil or demon for what we do seems like such a convenient way to try to escape personal responsibility.

A once-popular comedian became famous for a line mentioning the devil, which he often used in skits. "The devil made me do it," he would say when his character was accused of doing something wrong. He was really funny, but we could see that the character was self-deceived. Nobody was fooled, except the character.

John Wesley believed that there was more than a grain of truth, however, in the statement "The devil made me do it." The root of deviant behavior reaches deeply into the soil of spiritual influence. In his sermon "Of Evil Angels," Wesley says that both God and people have a common spiritual enemy, variously called "the devil," "the prince of this world," or "Satan." We are being naive if we write off this negative influence as a figment of the imagination or a form of superstition. No one today wants to repeat the rush to judgment of the Puritans, nor do we want to discount too quickly what the Bible teaches about spiritual forces of evil.

Wesley's notions of evil spiritual powers were much more sane than the notions we see in medieval paintings and sculpture. The devil, for Wesley, does not run around with a pitchfork in hand; neither does the evil one have a forked tail or hooves for feet. The subject is more serious that that. Wesley is speaking of forces for evil, which are often sophisticated, always calculating. In his sermons "The Mystery of Iniquity" and "National Sins and Miseries," John Wesley places the problems of society and church at the feet of evil powers. Wesley believed that the "mystery of our religion" (1 Timothy 3:16) is threatened by the "mystery of iniquity" (2 Thessalonians 2:7, King James Version). The struggle is personal, national, even cosmic. In his sermon "Satan's Devices," Wesley analyzes why people are sometimes so violently opposed to the preaching of Christian perfection, to the encouragement to love others with all one's heart. Wesley believed that such people are tricked; they are motivated and energized by evil; they are robbed of joy and hindered in their pursuit of God. In saying this, Wesley was not looking for a demon under every rock, nor was he saying people are not responsible for what they do. But he was saying in clear terms that the powers that opposed Jesus oppose his church today, and that we ignore these powers at our peril.

The Bible records at least two times in the life of Jesus when Jesus saw what was happening to him as the work of spiritual evil. One was at the time of his temptation by Satan, just before Jesus began his public ministry. The other, the one at which we will look, occurred when he was arrested at night in the garden of Gethsemane, just before his crucifixion. Judas, who was leading a group of authorities to arrest Jesus, betrayed the Lord with what was usually a kiss of peace and friendship. Then Jesus addressed his adversaries:

> Have you come out with swords and clubs as if I were a bandit? When I was with you day after day in the temple, you did not lay hands on me. But this is your hour, and the power of darkness!
> (Luke 22:52-53)

By "power of darkness," Jesus was referring to the moral darkness of those who were planning to kill him. Evil was reigning at that moment. Though powerful, this darkness would be short-lived because even that evil was working into God's larger design for the salvation of the world. The point is that radical evil ruled that hour. Evil was so strong that it put fear into the hearts of the disciples and they all, to a person, cowered during Jesus' trial and crucifixion. So forceful was this evil that only the strength of the Holy Spirit, granted to the apostles at Pentecost, could brace the disciples to stand against it. Jesus' experience with those who arrested him makes us cautious. When all the scholars and critics have spoken, what we know of the "mystery of iniquity" is a matter of revelation. But while its origins are clouded, its manifestations are often transparent in the troubles of the world.

The Deadly Sickness

In classical Greek theater, the stage was divided into two levels. The upper level was the realm of the gods; the lower was the land of mortals. Quite often the two levels had little to do with each other. The gods were often fighting and loving among themselves and paying no attention to the mortals below. Such a scene would have been strange indeed to the Hebrews. To them, what went on in the heavens had immense significance for human life. The interplay between the heavens and earth is at times so intense in Scripture that they blend into one. When our Lord spoke of "the power of darkness," as we read above, he was thinking of the influence of cosmic evil on earthly life. The devil might be separate from Jesus' enemies, but those enemies clearly did the devil's will. The judgment of God would therefore be leveled at two guilty parties: the devil himself and those who mimicked his intentions. Wesley also understood this interplay between evil spirits and evil people, and he warns us about it.

The church teaches that some people are motivated to do evil by spiritual powers outside themselves. This does not mean they necessarily hear voices or things such as that. But it does mean such people make evil choices largely because they are acting according to powerful temptations they feel. As much as the church values psychology, everything bad cannot be explained by an appeal to psychology alone. As we have seen, our liturgy of baptism draws attention to the human need to acknowledge and reject evil spiritual powers as part of our dedication to Christ. The fact that evil influence can be rejected is evidence to us that God in Christ is a much more powerful influence. Wesley wants us to recapture the early church's confidence that the power of the devil is seriously limited and will be completely overthrown in God's timing. In the meantime, we want to be well aware that evil seeks to destroy good, which complicates life considerably.

Evil is sometimes difficult for some modern Americans to imagine or discuss. Although we experience evil, we really have no common language with which to describe it. If we try to set aside religious and philosophical language, we are left without metaphors to describe what we know as a real truth: Evil exists and invades our lives. America has been described as a culture of irony, that is, a culture that has largely discredited traditional moral understandings and substituted in their place judgment without authority. We know there is "absurd evil," as one philosopher puts it, which is so out of the ordinary that it requires a new word to speak of it. We see this evil acted out in genocide, whether in Nazi Germany or, as I write, in modern Yugoslavia. But in combating evil, most of us rely on a vague sense of rightness and wrongness without the benefit of either God or Satan. This reductionism (reducing evil to simply right and wrong) robs us of meaningful ways to discuss the roots of genuine psychopathic evil. In my own research at the medical library at Vanderbilt University, I found that many papers written by psychiatrists and other therapists use the word *evil* as the only proper way to describe the behavior of some people. Their actions are that bad. The simple truth is that evil exists.

Some people try to explain evil as something of a void, something like the absence of meaning. It is as though there is a chasm in the human heart that is too wide to bridge. For more than a generation, many people have viewed life as a sort of cosmic happenstance, a strange combination of indifferent evolutionary forces with no design and no promise. To many, a sense of dread seems to hang over everything. Evil becomes the absence of good. In the mid-twentieth century, the Theater of the Absurd, as it was often called, promoted films and plays that interpreted life as essentially meaningless and filled with unexplainable evil. Life simply had to be endured. This is a powerful perspective on human existence, a kind of pessimism that can pervade every aspect of what we do. For these folks, there is no devil to "make us do it." From a Christian standpoint, however, this view is inadequate because it does not hold out the possibility of wholeness. Rather, evil as void is always there and always prevails. The greatest void, then, becomes death, which is inevitable. To us, the message of the gospel is that God overcomes evil, however one understands it, and brings happiness and hope in place of despair. The void can be avoided! The ultimate void of death has been conquered by love.

In his sermon "On Family Religion," John Wesley urges parents to be intentional in the moral training of their children. Children are easily influenced, so parents must help them learn good values, understand the fear of God, and develop skills to resist temptation. Helping children learn to say no to drugs, pornography, and crime is a must. Like it or not, Wesley is absolutely right in saying that evil lurks around the family, looking for ways to destroy this basic social unit. For Wesley, being a good example of love and compassion and of strength and dependability is absolutely necessary in training children to serve God and avoid the pitfalls of rebellion. Family therapists echo Wesley's advice, since much evidence suggests that antisocial behavior can be set in a child's mind and actions as early as age four. Why would a drug pusher want to turn your innocent child into an addict? Because, says Wesley, the pusher manifests in his or her life the evil intentions of the great enemy of God, whether the pusher understands it that way or not.

Though he saw great evil in his society, Wesley could not have envisioned our world and the continual threat of gigantic moral calamity that we face. The specter of tribal warfare in some countries, the shadow of the Holocaust and other projects of genocide, random violence, the deliberate making of germ and other biological munitions for war, and the strange rituals of satanic cults are all evidences of broader influences of evil, more than can be attributed to bad family upbringing, trying economic conditions, stunted social life, and psychological disturbance. There is a will to evil.

In a recent telecast on crime in America, the host remarked that we live in the age of the serial killer. These sociopaths—such as Ted Bundy, who confessed to murdering more than twenty females and is suspected in many more cases, and Jeffrey Dahmer, the "Milwaukee Monster"—are real-life incarnations of Hannibal Lecter of the movie and book *The Silence of the Lambs*. This is a modern image of Satan, a being that swallows up good in its own twisted desire to control. The Wesleys warn us that much of the problem we face is spiritual and that the victory of the resurrected Christ is destined to ensure that peace will reign instead of chaos, and goodness instead of badness.

Using medical language, the Wesleys often say societies are diseased; they are sick. This view of culture was shared by many Protestants in the seventeenth century; today many, even outside the Christian faith, believe that to be true. Albert Camus, a great twentieth-century writer and social critic, agreed with Wesley. The main theme of Camus' famous book *The Plague* is that so-called civilized societies suffer from a kind of deadly plague. The bubonic plague, carried by rats, comes to the peaceful city of Oran in Algiers, and the entire city is infected. The city must be quarantined as people die in misery in the streets and in their homes. It is an awful scene. For Camus, the plague was a symbol of human greed and violence. In a similar way, John Wesley saw society as an infected and infecting reality. Christians must be careful or they, even unintentionally, will be infected. If we play around with the evil that surrounds us, we may well die. Our belief that we can control evil, that we can give in to some of its temptations without giving in completely, is a monstrous deception.

We should not be surprised to learn that Wesley advised us to be careful who we marry and with whom we do business. While it is not possible to separate oneself from all contact with society, we can minimize how much we have to do with people who are a problem for us. The writer of Psalm 1 understood this and began his poem in this way: "Happy are those who do not follow the advice of the wicked, or take the path that sinners tread, or sit in the seat of scoffers." A popular mode of evangelism today suggests striking up a relationship with non-Christian people. This is good, but the evangelist has to keep her or his life in balance. While the Lord ate with sinners in a culture valuing hospitality as a means of identification, Jesus also warned the crowd in the Sermon on the Mount to be wise in relating to others. The crux of the issue for Wesley is that if we do not influence others positively, we run the risk of being influenced negatively by them.

Temptation: A Common Test

To the Corinthians Paul wrote: "No testing has overtaken you that is not common to everyone. God is faithful, and he will not let you be tested beyond your strength, but with the testing he will also provide the way out so that you may be able to endure it" (1 Corinthians 10:13). Temptation is common. This saying reflects on Israel's past, for the Hebrews had doubted God's promise to provide for them in the wilderness and had failed to keep faith. Paul wants us to learn from their mistake. This is the basic issue with temptation from the perspective of the New Testament: Temptation is always a test of faith and value. In the New Testament sense, temptation is not being encouraged to eat a little more cake, with the prospect of adding a pound or two; rather, it is a matter of the life or death of the spirit.

John Wesley's sermon "On Temptation" is about Paul's statement to the Corinthians. Wesley, who was eighty-three years old at the time, was concerned about people making professions of faith and then falling away. As an evangelist, he saw a lot of people begin well but end in disaster. This does not have to happen; falling is not inevitable. Wesley understood that temptations come from several directions: from the spiritual powers of evil, from the natural weakness of the body, from nature gone wild (earthquakes, tornadoes, floods), and from other people (including our friends). One of the problems of our life that we cannot change is that we live amid "the ruins of a disordered world."[1] As Charles Wesley puts it in a hymn:

> What mighty troubles hast thou shown
>   Thy feeble, tempted followers here!
> We have through fire and water gone.[2]

The Wesleys were realists. They knew what many would like to forget: The followers of the Lord always live with great risk. This was especially true of the Methodists. In St. Ives, England, the police stood by and watched an angry mob ransack Methodist homes and beat up Methodist people. Such brutality was all too common. John Wesley was literally attacked at times by people who felt threatened by the Revival Movement. This persecution produced widely varying results. Some people were strengthened in their resolve to follow Christ; others simply gave up under the pressure. They were like the "lapsed" in the early church; they could not stand trial. This still happens today at the office and at school. Anticipating what may happen, however, will strengthen us in the event that it does. We need to be wise.

We all know from experience that outward temptations, however rough and recurring, can gain no ground unless they find a willing heart. Ministers are taught that when dealing with people under severe temptation, they should take into account such things as how our identities are formed and how family systems influence that shaping, as well as theological understandings of human nature. The same can be said for ministers who find themselves under temptation. Wesley knew that we can be helped by God to withstand temptation, but not even God can keep us from sin if we want to give in to temptation.

Everyone must therefore endure temptation. Our temptations can become opportunities to grow or to self-destruct. Wesley puts it this way: As Christians, our center is God; of that there can be no dispute. Wesley means that our firm intention is to love God and live out that love in our lives. We want to love God not as a wish but as an actuality. To want to love God means that we set an agenda. It may be that we will increase our devotional life, be more regular in attending worship, or serve on a community committee trying to help the poor. What it does not mean is saying "I want to love God more" and then doing nothing. If a mother says she wants to learn more about her child, then she does what is necessary to learn more about that child. Christian life is no mere wish; it is action.

The idea of temptation can be seen positively as well as negatively. As in the case of Job, temptation comes more as a test in which Job has an opportunity of demonstrating his steadfastness. So far we have been looking at temptation more in the manner of James 1:13-16:

> No one, when tempted, should say, "I am being tempted by God"; for God cannot be tempted by evil and he himself tempts no one. But one is tempted by one's own desire, being lured and enticed by it; then, when that desire has conceived, it gives birth to sin, and that sin, when it is fully grown, gives birth to death. Do not be deceived, my beloved.

Wesley believed that it is when we turn away from our center in God that we get into real trouble. In his sermon "On Dissipation," John Wesley warns us not to become "distracted" from God. For Wesley, this is to turn again to our old loves (before we were serious Christians), such as focusing on our career, on gaining more pleasure, or, in the case of a minister, to turning from the spirit of religion to its form. Whatever shape temptation takes, it is always a temptation to doubt God's goodness. Such seeds of doubt about God's love and care could easily spread to total unbelief. It need not, but it could. Surely you know someone, maybe yourself, who at one time thoroughly loved God, but gradually let that excitement and devotion weaken. Temptation comes in many forms—and temptation must come—but it is not necessary that we fall because of it. Paul encouraged the Corinthians by telling them that, though they were tempted, God would not let them fall if they did not want to fall.

A State of War

The apostle Paul wrote to the Christians at Ephesus that they should regard their Christian life as warfare against evil. That is an ominous metaphor, especially to people of peace. To make peace, Jesus said, is to be godlike. No word is more odious for people of peace than *war*. This is especially true for people in an age overwhelmed with nuclear weaponry, the very existence of which precludes any reasonable idea of limited war. The destructive capability of such weaponry dredges up frightening images of wreckage, both human and material. For Paul, the notion of war adequately represents the clash of wills that goes on between the person who would do good and the forces seemingly arrayed against her or him. However repugnant the idea of war may be to Christians, it is nonetheless a realistic image for life in the world.

> Finally, be strong in the Lord and in the strength of his power. Put on the whole armor of God, so that you may be able to stand against the wiles of the devil. For our struggle is not against enemies of blood and flesh, but against the rulers, against the authorities, against the cosmic powers of this present darkness, against the spiritual forces of evil in the heavenly places.
>
> (Ephesians 6:10-12)

The apostle goes on to line out the various parts of a Roman soldier's frontal armor, spiritualizing them as representative of the seriousness of the war Christians are in every day.

Charles Wesley wrote a long, three-part (twelve-stanza) hymn based on Paul's advice to the Ephesians. Four of the stanzas have been combined into the well-known hymn "Soldiers of Christ, Arise." Two stanzas, published in *Hymns,* are worth noting here:

> Stand then against your foes
> In close and firm array;
> Legions of wily fiends oppose
> Throughout the evil day;
> But meet the sons of night,
> But mock their vain design,
> Armed in the arms of heavenly light,
> Of righteousness divine.
>
> Leave no unguarded place,
> No weakness of the soul;
> Take every virtue, every grace,
> And fortify the whole;
> Indissolubly joined,
> To battle all proceed,
> But arm yourselves with all the mind
> That was in Christ your head.[3]

These two stanzas summarize the situation: The enemy are "your foes," "wily fiends," and "sons of night." They fight Christians ("in close and firm array") "throughout the evil day." Remember our Lord's words on the night of his betrayal, quoted above (page 30), about it being the "hour [of] the power of darkness"? The enemy are "legions" of these tempters. (Wesley is referring to Mark 5:9 and Luke 8:30, in which a man called himself Legion for the number of demons inside him. A Roman legion consisted of up to six thousand men!) The word *legions* means that the odds against believers are overwhelming. Yet the church is to meet these staggering forces head on, even "mocking" their intention to destroy the church of Jesus. Christians lean on Jesus' promise that the "gates" (powers) of hell will not overcome the church (Matthew 16:18).

The certainty of the promise of the Lord does not mean that Christians can be cocky. We are, says Wesley, to enter this battle of the spirit wholly fortified for it. We are to have the "mind" of Christ as our weapon ("arm yourselves"), to be sure that there is no inner weakness in our life, to be virtuous, and to be joined to each other as members of Christ, our "head" (Ephesians 1:22-23). This is not works-righteousness; Christians cannot go it alone. We are totally dependent on the living Lord (and the community of faith) for our progress in faith. Anything less than faith is misplaced confidence and is doomed to failure.

I have talked with Christians who have felt at times as I do—that is, asking why we must struggle so in a life that is described as peaceful. The truth is that much of the time we do not feel at peace, but struggle with dilemmas such as relational problems, job opportunities that require uprooting the family, or even the worry of how the utility bill is going to be paid. If nothing else, the hot water heater goes out on a weekend or the car breaks down fifty miles from nowhere. I have heard it said that how we react to a situation is more important than the situation itself. There is a grain of common sense—and Christian grace—in that statement. Following Jesus may not keep us from severe trials—indeed, we may have trials because of him—but Christ enables us to keep perspective. I am aware, of course, of the Christian family whose child is abducted or traumatized in some other serious way. I have seen mothers, fathers, and children in desperate circumstances emerge with hope and confidence in God.

The apostle Paul warns us not to give in to the flesh, but rather to walk in the Spirit. What is the flesh? Paul speaks of the flesh as actions that are lustful, divisive, judgmental. Followers of the Lord can and do slip into patterns of behavior that are harmful to themselves and others, which is one of the reasons Paul urges us to check ourselves occasionally to be sure we are still keeping the faith. If we are not careful, we can become insensitive, if not injurious, to a spouse, a child, an employee, a friend.

An example of how Christians can unwittingly justify bad behavior happened to me in Southern California. During a talk on interpersonal relationships at a church, I mentioned that Christians should work to create a climate of trust and kindness to all races of people. Within a couple days I received a letter from one of the people who had attended the conference. She included in her letter some anti-Semitic literature, which was supposedly written by a Christian author. Her letter suggested a sincere desire to follow Christ, but the social shape of her faith was wrong; it was not at all in keeping with the Lord of the Gospels.

Wesley recognized that we bring many family and other social influences into our faith, some of which may actually work against our faith. Paul writes of this as a conflict between "flesh" and "Spirit" (Galatians 5:17). The Holy Spirit creates life, love, peace, good will, and compassion. The flesh, which is really self-serving, perpetuates separateness, suspicion, indifference, and harshness. All of us struggle with the job of bringing our attitudes and actions in line with the Spirit of the Lord. It seems like a never-ending task; yet few things are as rewarding as becoming a kinder, gentler person. The Holy Spirit enables us to work with Christ, not against him.

Behaviors come from within us. Sometimes we are kind and thoughtful; at other times we are defensive and selfish. All of us have uttered words we later wished we had not said, or have given that look we wished we could take back. We feel guilty because we know, sometimes immediately, that what we did was a betrayal of our most-cherished Christian commitments. None of us is exempt from this kind of thing. A friend of mine who is a minister once made an obscene gesture at another motorist who had cut him off abruptly in heavy traffic. It just happened. His teenage son, who was sitting in the passenger's seat, yelled, "Dad!" His son's reaction shocked him into realizing what he had just done. As you can imagine, no good explanation was possible. The sagging feeling my friend had was an indication that he had a lot of probing to do and a lot of adjustments to make. The good thing is that the negative stuff in us can be brought to Christ for forgiveness and correction. The call to holy living always challenges us to be what we profess.

Concluding Thoughts

As Christians, we are keenly aware of the world around us, including its natural beauty and its unnatural attractions. We have seen that the Wesleys viewed the life of faith as a battle against destructive spiritual and human forces. Not only are we at times in conflict with evil in other people and always in conflict with the demonic, but we also have to struggle with our own desires when they contradict God's will. It seems strange that personal and social holiness come at a high price; yet the gospel message is that Christ died and rose that we might die to evil and rise to goodness. In order to do this successfully, we need Wesley's insight on what we can do to become "altogether a Christian."[4] The next chapter will open the door for us on spiritual disciplines that will benefit us as we make our way to the kingdom of God's grace.

Probing Our Faith

1. Sometimes we try to escape responsibility by blaming others for our wrong actions. How does Jesus' parable of the great dinner (Luke 14:15-24) speak to this?
2. The prophet Hosea said sin is like a terrible sickness (6:1). Jesus announced that part of his ministry was to heal sinners (Luke 5:31-32). What would it mean to be healed of sin?
3. Spiritual teachers often say that temptation can be a means of growth in our faith. Would you agree with this? Why do you answer as you do?
4. Where in your life does being a Christian cause tension? How do you handle that?

ENDNOTES

1 From "On Temptation," in *The Works of John Wesley*, Volume 3, edited by Albert C. Outler, page 160. © 1986 Abingdon Press. Used by permission.

2 From "For the Society, Meeting," in *The Works of John Wesley*, Volume 7, edited by Franz Hildebrandt and Oliver A. Beckerlegge, with the assistance of James Dale, page 655. © 1983 Abingdon Press. Used by permission.

3 From "For Believers Fighting," in *The Works of John Wesley*, Volume 7, edited by Franz Hildebrandt and Oliver A. Beckerlegge, with the assistance of James Dale, pages 399–400. © 1983 Abingdon Press. Used by permission.

4 From "The Almost Christian," in *The Works of John Wesley*, Volume 1, edited by Albert C. Outler, page 131. © 1984 Abingdon Press. Used by permission.

Chapter 3

Growing in God's Love

ew human experiences are as devastating as starvation. Some years ago my wife, Ruth, went with others from our church on a trip to the country of Belize to help refurbish part of a church. While cleaning a Sunday school room, she found a rather large piece of crumpled-up brown paper in a corner. When she straightened it out, she found a heartbreaking poem on poverty that had been written by one of the local children. At the time, Belize was a rather poor country, so it was easy to see how a child would write about such a difficult subject.

The four-stanza poem spoke movingly about children who had nothing to eat, children whose skin was as thin as paper. The poem depicted little boys and girls with hollow eyes and protruding bones begging in the streets. They were kids with no hope, and begging was all they could do. This little poet sadly said that without money for a doctor and something to stem their hunger, they would soon die. The poem has haunted me for years. Who could read it and not have his or her heart pierced? The poem speaks of a tragedy that stalks the modern world. In spite of wealth and technology, millions of people are starving and, unless help comes, will die unwanted and forgotten.

We face a similar tragedy at home and abroad, but it is not quite so obvious. It is a starvation of the spirit, and it is in every way as serious as starvation of the body. It happens whenever women and men are abused and their sense of self-worth decays. It also happens in the spiritual life when people's faith begins to die for lack of inner nourishment. No one knew of this possibility more than the people of Israel, for their sins kept God from speaking to them (Amos 8:11). Later, in the New Testament, the mature Paul cautions the immature Timothy about being influenced by the wrong crowd (2 Timothy 3) because he wants Timothy to keep his spirit healthy. Our Lord warns us to keep faith and "enter through the narrow gate" (Matthew 7:13-23). The Wesleys, too, saw many instances of believers whose faith was, to borrow from Paul the apostle, "shipwrecked" (1 Timothy 1:19). According to the Bible, losing one's physical life is terrible, but losing one's spiritual life is unspeakable (Luke 9:25).

In recent years, the church has placed a great deal of emphasis on spiritual growth. We are learning that like moving from infancy to old age, spiritual life also progresses through stages. None of us is born into the Kingdom as full-fledged spiritual adults. The New Testament speaks of some believers as babes in Christ, others as mature adults, some even as soldiers. Becoming mature in faith takes time and desire. Our growth in Christ is the result of trial and error, dedication to the goal of being like Christ, and struggle with adversity (just as Christ did). This process is really nothing new to us. Everyone reading these pages has at one time or another begun some new phase of life, not as an accomplished and polished veteran but as a novice or apprentice. Advancement came as the result of hard work and self-denial, of work with others and acceptance of correction. This is the way in any career, and this is the way of becoming a follower of Jesus Christ. Determination and dedication are necessary to avoid the shipwreck of the soul.

Although many models of spiritual growth have been proposed, these models tend to follow the same general path: We begin by coming into faith through repentance and conversion. This is followed by learning about the faith and reshaping our life to conform to the new standards we received in baptism. We begin to learn about prayer, and the Scriptures come alive to us. We gather with others to worship and to become involved in our church and community. We learn some difficult lessons about ourselves: We have many flaws and are not the perfect people we once thought we were. We grow because God is working with us constantly. The older we become in faith, the

less judgmental we become and the more open we are to the influence of spiritual books and friends. We pass through dark periods of
trial and learn to trust God when we have no religious feelings. Joy in
our faith deepens over time, and death becomes less of a threat.
God's love gradually takes over more and more of our lives, and love
becomes the standard for what we do. If we live long enough, we
become spiritual grandparents, so to speak. We learn to sit lightly on
our possessions, and heaven opens up as our natural destiny.

This "way of faith"[1] comes to us as God's gift. God helps us
believe and increase in that belief. God shows us that the highest
thing we can know is unselfconscious love, which is when we spontaneously reach out to God with adoration and praise and to others
without thought of personal reward or recognition. Undoubtedly,
the greatest fruit of our growth is the turning of our will from self-
interest to self-giving. The apostle Paul writes of this as having the
"same mind…that was in Christ Jesus," a mind of humility and
obedience to God without question (Philippians 2:5-11). It is easy
to see that this life, however desirable and appealing, cannot be
gained unless we put heart and soul into it. None of us can have a
flourishing spiritual life without personal discipline.

In this chapter, we will look at John Wesley's teaching on the
"means of grace"[2] as the normal way God uses to bring our lives
under the Spirit's control. Remember, our goal is always holiness
and happiness in heart and life. The means of grace, particularly
prayer, Scripture, and the Lord's Supper, lead us deeper and deeper
into our new life in Christ. This chapter will help prepare us for
the next chapter, which emphasizes the social responsibilities of
holy living. This chapter on growing in God will also be important
for a future chapter on the church as the nurturing atmosphere for
spiritual growth.

We Belong to God

Regardless of the circumstances of your birth, you are special to
God. Silver spoon in your mouth or no spoon at all, God loves
you with an eternal love and wants you to know, to feel, to experience that love. Have you noticed how tender Jesus is toward the

hurting people he meets? The Lord soothes people's pain, whether physical or emotional. He once raised a woman's only son from death and gave him back to his mother. He touched the blind eyes of a beggar and restored his sight. He forgave the sins of a repentant woman who bathed his feet with her tears and dried them with her hair. Over and over again the Lord assured people that they counted, that their lives were precious to God. Jesus loves the starving children, too. Only the arrogant and judgmental stood against him, trying to stop his mission of kindness, redemption, and revelation. As we begin to look at Wesley's suggestions on how we can grow in God, we need to remember that we are important to God and were created to be with God eternally. Our faith teaches that we were in God's mind from the very beginning.

Speaking on Psalm 8:4 ("What are human beings that you are mindful of them, mortals that you care for them?"), John Wesley says that the reason we were created by God is so we can "know" God now and "enjoy" God forever.[3] Wesley urges us to remember that this is the very reason we were born in the first place. Sometimes we may wonder why we are even here on earth. You are not here by accident; you are here because God wanted you here. And as important as our family, friends, and career are to us, Wesley says we do not live for any of those relationships alone; we live for God, who made us and gave us breath. Everyone can succeed at this—that is, all of us can love God with all our hearts and do God's will in all that we do. Like other reformers before him, John Wesley believed that our true life and destiny are wrapped up in God. God complements our deepest desires.

To be created by God as a thinking and feeling person is a wonderful thing. Biblical writers say we are created in God's "image." This is usually understood to mean that we can love, be responsible, and make decisions to change our behavior. The image of God in us has to do with that special quality of being a reflecting and caring person. It is God who makes this happen. God wants to share the Holy Spirit with us so that we can be loving. The qualities of excellence that are seen in God can be duplicated in our lives. We were created to grow, to change by moving "from faith to faith."[4] As Wesley said, we were born to enjoy God, now and forever.

The Means of Grace

The next time you are in your favorite bookstore, take a good look at the books in the self-help section. You will see many publications designed to help you deal with the most common experiences of life. In addition to books on losing weight, you will find popular books on controlling anger, getting along better with your spouse, dealing with abusive relationships (including the boss who does not understand), and figuring out who you are and what you should be doing. Yet, in spite of the many books that have been written over the years to help us with the basic questions of life, we still deal with the same kinds of essential problems that haunted our grandparents: *How can I cope with loss? Does anyone out there love me? What about tomorrow? Where is God? Can I speak to God?*

We should not be surprised, then, to find books on personal growth in the religion section of the bookstore. Even common questions have to be raised and answered anew for every generation. Lately, books on devotional life have become popular with Christians. Many of the old classics are being reprinted, and spiritual masters from the past are speaking today with a new clarity. For example, two authors who influenced the young Wesley are still available. *The Imitation of Christ,* by Thomas à Kempis, and *The Practice of the Presence of God,* by Brother Lawrence, help thousands to a more fruitful life with God. They helped Wesley explore the idea that faith and love are the basic working principles of everyday life.

If we were to try to sum up Wesley's view of salvation, we could do so with the word *grace.* In the Bible, *grace* connects with other words such as *mercy, love, forgiveness, goodness, kindness,* and *justice.* We can say that God is "grace-full." Or we can say that God loves to give goodness to us. You see, God's nature floods our lives with kindness and mercy. Wesley was convinced that we do not deserve such indescribable love. Wesley was—and is still—right. God does not give us grace because we deserve it, but because God wants to give us grace and we need it. Wesley said we can do nothing to earn God's grace. Wesley is right, but we do not have to earn grace. Just looking in God's direction is to receive grace to make us good, merciful, and forgiving. Means of grace are God-appointed ways of helping us look more intently in God's direction.

John Wesley occasionally wrote about "works of piety."[5] Those words are outdated for us, but the concept is up-to-date. Wesley means that if we are to grow in likeness to God, then we need to develop a regular devotional life. We know that the word *Methodist* was given as a spiteful term to the early followers of Wesley. Why? Because they were so methodical in their worship and work. By having prayers at a set time and by visiting the sick, the poor, and the prisoners regularly, the Wesleys and their friends were saying that holy routine is important to growth in God. This is not magic; rather, these are things our Lord urges us to do. For John Wesley, the main ways God comes to us are through (1) prayer, (2) Scripture, and (3) the Lord's Supper.

Prayer as a means of grace. Note that prayer is the first thing on Wesley's list. What is prayer? The Wesleys understood prayer as conversation with God. That does not mean talking constantly; rather, it is more like being with someone, such as a spouse or best friend. That presence is as great as, and sometimes greater, than words. Listen to Charles Wesley speak about closeness with God. Do you sense the intimacy in this stanza?

> I want a heart to pray,
>   To pray and never cease,
> Never to murmur at thy stay,
>   Or wish my sufferings less.
>   This blessing above all,
>   Always to pray I want,
> Out of the deep on thee to call,
>   And never, never faint.[6]

Much of what prayer is about is found in these words. Wesley talks about a desire in us to pray, about being willing to do what God wants, of the need to stress prayer in our daily life, and to pray even when we do not feel like it. All of these elements are important in our relationship with the Lord. Our Lord Jesus encourages us to talk with God. Wesley quotes from Jesus' Sermon on the Mount: "Ask, and it shall be given you; seek, and ye shall find; knock, and it shall be opened unto you." Then Wesley writes: "Here,...in the plainest manner,"[7] we are taught to pray, and to pray expectantly.

The most perfect form of prayer is the Lord's Prayer. This prayer, Wesley maintains, "contains all we can reasonably or innocently desire,"[8] both for ourselves and for anyone we know. John Wesley devoted considerable time to looking carefully at the Lord's Prayer and to showing its relevance to our lives. I will summarize some of his insights for you, which you may think about the next time you pray the Lord's Prayer.

Our Father, who art in heaven, ➝ God is good and willing to hear our prayers.

hallowed be thy name. ➝ Let us bless the name of God, recognizing God's greatness.

Thy kingdom come, ➝ May God's kingdom of grace be known among us and God's kingdom of glory come quickly to all.

thy will be done ➝ Our desire as God's children is to do God's will above our own in everything.

on earth as it is in heaven. ➝ May God's will be done willingly, continually, and perfectly by all, especially in showing mercy.

Give us this day our daily bread. ➝ Give us our daily needs and the sacrament of the Lord's Supper as well, so that we may grow physically and spiritually.

And forgive us our trespasses, ➝ Only God can forgive sin, so we turn to God alone.

as we forgive those who trespass against us. ➝ God forgives us to the same extent we forgive others.

And lead us not into temptation, ➝ Lead us safely through our many trials and temptations.

but deliver us from evil. ➝ Fill our hearts with peace and joy, heaven and God.

For thine is the kingdom, and the power, and the glory, forever. ➝ No one is like God.

Amen.[9] ➝ Let this prayer be true in us, O Blessed Trinity.

To pray in this way is to pray the right way. The Wesleys want us to form a habit of conversing with God about everything. This is a way of living that John Wesley read about in the writings of Brother Lawrence, a seventeenth-century monk with keen insight. We also need to remember that what we want is God's will to be done, so that we do not dictate what that will be. We come to God with boldness, lay our petitions before God, and patiently wait for the pleasure of God's will. Preaching on the Lord's Prayer, John Wesley said we sometimes try to inform God about things, as though God did not know already; but actually we are informing ourselves about our readiness to do God's will. We are also not trying to move God in the direction we want, but learning to trust God's rock-solid love to do what is best for us and for those about whom we are concerned. Such praying is confident of God's care, even when things seem to be going badly.

The Wesleys even bring the Lord's Supper into their teaching on the Lord's Prayer by mentioning the Great Thanksgiving, the words prayed at the consecration of the bread and wine. This one prayer catches up the history of God's saving acts, the joyful response of God's people, the gracious life of Jesus, the night of Christ's betrayal, the giving of the gifts (of bread and wine), the coming of the Spirit to bless, the confidence of the church in Jesus, and the unity of the church's life and witness. The Great Thanksgiving in the service of Word and Table is a splendid prayer, all-inclusive of God's love for the world and the response of those who have "[tasted] the goodness"[10] of the Lord. (We will learn more about the Lord's Supper later in this chapter.) Actually, all our worship is a form of prayer in one way or another as we praise, petition, and give thanks to God, the Father, Son, and Holy Spirit.

Scripture as a means of grace. From the outset of my Christian life, I knew that Scripture was important. I had no view of the inspiration of the Bible; I just sensed that if I wanted to know what the faith was about, I would have to study the Bible. To this day I have devoted myself to studying the Sacred Text and apply-ing it to my life. As much as I have read it (particularly the Gospels and the Psalms), taught it to my students in preaching and theology classes, and preached from it to congregations, I still have a sense that whenever I open those pages, some new insight is going to come to me. I feel a kinship with John Wesley when I read in the introduction to his short commentary on the New Testament that Scripture is a fountain of holy wisdom from which we drink. The confidence that God is going to come to us in the study of the Scriptures is what Wesley means when he calls the Bible a means of grace.

It may worry some to note that of the three chief means of grace, the Bible comes second on the list. Prayer is first. What do you think that means? The Wesleys seem to be saying that God as God comes before the Bible as God's word. The Bible, whatever else it is, is a gift, a collection of sacred writings in narrative, poetry, prophecy, and teaching that speaks to the central themes of God's love for the world. True, the Christian faith is a faith of a book; yet it is more than that. The book is not supreme; God alone is supreme. Prayer's place as primary means that an intimate relationship with God is what matters most. Of course, the Bible helps shape that relationship by providing information and inspiration. We must have it!

We need to keep in mind that in order to understand the Scriptures spiritually, we must ask God to help us. In his hymn (which is a prayer) "Before Reading the Scriptures," Charles Wesley asks the Holy Spirit for assistance. The second stanza is really important for us:

> Come, Holy Ghost (for moved by thee
>   The prophets wrote and spoke);
> Unlock the truth, thyself the key,
>   Unseal the sacred book.[11]

While the Wesleys often appealed to reason in settling disputes and discussing Christian beliefs, they never appealed to reason apart from faith. The Wesleys knew that however wonderful our natural capacity to think things through and to apply logic in solving problems, we can never reason our way to God. In understanding divine things (ways and knowledge), we need divine help. We should therefore read the Bible with openness and humility.

Do you have a favorite biblical book? John Wesley's favorite was Matthew. (Some 1,362 references to this Gospel are found in his sermons). Yet Wesley used Mark 1:15 ("The time is fulfilled, and the kingdom of God has come near; repent, and believe in the good news") more than any other passage as a text for preaching. Wesley also liked the Old Testament books Isaiah and Psalms. His favorite text from the Old Testament was Isaiah 55:7.[12]

> Let the wicked forsake their way,
>   and the unrighteous their thoughts;
> let them return to the LORD,
>   that he may have mercy on them,
> and to our God, for he will
>   abundantly pardon.

Wesley was a master of the common Greek text. While Wesley called himself a "Bible-bigot,"[13] he strengthened his appreciation of Scripture with strict attention to the classics (particularly from Western civilization) and to the writings of Christian antiquity. He was well-read and comfortable in several languages. Charles Wesley was also knowledgeable about the Bible. Both brothers believed that God's gifts of grace often come to us in the Bible. If we do not study Scripture and take it to heart, how can we hope to grow in spiritual awareness and hope against the trials of life? The words of Jesus (in the four Gospels) are particularly helpful as we seek to know God and learn how to live God's way.

The Lord's Supper as a means of grace. I have heard some describe the Lord's Supper as the Cinderella of the Methodist Movement, a beautiful princess waiting to be recognized. If this is true, it would shock the Wesleys, because that is precisely what was happening in much of the Anglican Church of their day. In fact, the Wesleyan Revival helped restore Holy Communion— another name for the Lord's Supper—to its place of importance in worship. According to John Wesley, we do more than just remember Jesus in the Lord's Supper; it is also a means of grace. By that Wesley means that God "conveys" (or puts) in our hearts God's marvelous love as we observe this sacrament. The next time you receive the Lord's Supper, think of it as God acting in your own heart in mysterious ways that produce joy and peace.[14]

Undoubtedly, at this point John Wesley's harshest critics take their best shots at him. Their complaint? Wesley was too Roman

Catholic for Protestant England. But Wesley was neither Protestant nor Catholic in any partisan way of speaking; he borrowed from both sides in his desire to find God. In addition, he dipped heavily into the Eastern Orthodox tradition. Wesley saw beauty and truth in everyone and refused to be cut off from the best expressions of genuine faith, wherever he found them. We can take a lesson from him here.

Jesus' telling his disciples to eat the bread and drink the cup "in remembrance" of him was enough for the Wesleys to insist that a renewal of faith must include a renewal of appreciation for this unique "supper." One of Charles Wesley's fine hymns for Holy Communion, "O the Depth of Love Divine" (*The United Methodist Hymnal,* 627), takes us into the mystery of the relationship between the spiritual and the material. In it, he poses a question: How can we possibly understand how God uses bread and wine to give us grace to live? Charles Wesley never answers that question. It just hangs in the air, for he knew it was an unanswerable question. So Wesley simply affirms the church's confidence that in this sacred meal God reaches out to us in love.

Notice the mystery in this hymn and in this celebration—this act of "Holy Mystery," as the Orthodox say. When the early Methodists celebrated Holy Communion, they invited everyone to the table if their hearts were seeking God. Any spiritual need could be met there if the heart was right. Some people were converted, others assured of their relationship with God, still others moved more deeply into the fullness of love. Holy Communion is a "universal feast" for all people to meet all needs. But Holy Communion is not magical. Rather, we look to God and to God's Son, who instituted this supper, for the spiritual life we need. Look again at the wonderful teaching of this hymn: God's love is beyond calculating; God comes to us under bread and wine; God's grace is real to save; we are bound together in the mystery of God's coming; we stand in awe of God's gracious working. As the hymn asks, what else is there? There is only one thing: to witness to others that they might share this grace unbounded and joy unspeakable.

Concluding Thoughts

According to John Wesley, other means of grace help us to God, but the three we have studied are primary. Did you notice that prayer, the use of Scripture, and Holy Communion are all a significant part of public worship? It makes sense, doesn't it? Where prayers come from the depths of the heart, where Scripture is interpreted in a relevant way, and where the family of God and genuine seekers think on Christ's sacrifice and coming again in Holy Communion, our hearts grow in love for God and one another. There—precisely there—grace abounds! The inward self is replenished for good works, and the fellowship of Christians grows in love.

The primary end of spiritual growth is the adoration of God. Whatever we do for ourselves and for others has this as its ultimate goal. May God help us to be strong, growing Christians. Let us give ourselves to becoming mature people of God, seeking God's holy love and living in God's holy ways. What this means for the people around us will be our concern in the next chapter.

Probing Our Faith

1. *The United Methodist Hymnal,* like other hymnals, is designed to be a prayer book as well as a songbook. Leaf through it, noting its divisions, prayers, and psalm readings. How can you use the *Hymnal* in your devotional life?

2. Wesley says we were created to "know, love, and serve God on earth, and enjoy him to all eternity."[15] As you think about your life with God, what do the words *know, love, serve,* and *enjoy* mean to you?

3. Some Christians have difficulty praying. Why would we find talking to God troubling, and what can we do to find joy in prayer?

The following prayer by Charles Wesley has to do with our need for God's strength. Meditate on the prayer and see how it can help you better cope with life's troubles.

Arm me with thy whole armour, Lord!
    Support my weakness with thy might;
Gird on my thigh thy conqu'ring sword,
    And shield me in the threatening fight:
From faith to faith, from grace to grace,
    So in thy strength shall I go on;
Till heaven and earth flee from thy face,
    And glory end what grace begun.[16]

ENDNOTES

1 From "Upon Our Lord's Sermon on the Mount, V," in *The Works of John Wesley,* Volume 1, edited by Albert C. Outler, page 560. © 1984 Abingdon Press. Used by permission.

2 From "The Means of Grace," in *The Works of John Wesley,* Volume 1, edited by Albert C. Outler, page 381. © 1984 Abingdon Press. Used by permission.

3 See "What Is Man?" in *The Works of John Wesley,* Volume 4, edited by Albert C. Outler (Nashville: Abingdon Press, 1987), page 26.

4 From "For Believers Rejoicing," in *The Works of John Wesley,* Volume 7, edited by Franz Hildebrandt and Oliver A. Beckerlegge, with the assistance of James Dale, page 318. © 1983 Abingdon Press. Used by permission.

5 From "Upon Our Lord's Sermon on the Mount, VI," in *The Works of John Wesley,* Volume 1, edited by Albert C. Outler, page 575. © 1984 Abingdon Press. Used by permission.

6 From "For Believers Praying," in *The Works of John Wesley,* Volume 7, edited by Franz Hildebrandt and Oliver A. Beckerlegge, with the assistance of James Dale, page 445. © 1983 Abingdon Press. Used by permission.

7 From "The Means of Grace," in *The Works of John Wesley,* Volume 1, edited by Albert C. Outler, page 384. © 1984 Abingdon Press. Used by permission.

8 From "Upon Our Lord's Sermon on the Mount, VI," in *The Works of John Wesley,* Volume 1, edited by Albert C. Outler, page 578. © 1984 Abingdon Press. Used by permission.

9 "From the Ritual of the Former Methodist Church," in *The United Methodist Hymnal* (Nashville: The United Methodist Publishing House, 1989), 895.

10 From "Come, Sinners, to the Gospel Feast," by Charles Wesley, in *The United Methodist Hymnal* (Nashville: The United Methodist Publishing House, 1989), 616.

11 From "Praying for a Blessing," in *The Works of John Wesley,* Volume 7, edited by Franz Hildebrandt and Oliver A. Beckerlegge, with the assistance of James Dale, page 185. © 1983 Abingdon Press. Used by permission.

12 See "Wesley and His Sources," in *The Works of John Wesley,* Volume 1, edited by Albert C. Outler (Nashville: Abingdon Press, 1984), page 69.

13 From "An Extract of the Rev. Mr. John Wesley's Journal, From May 27, 1765 to May 18, 1768," in *The Works of John Wesley,* Volume 22, edited by W. Reginald Ward and Richard P. Heitzenrater, page 42. © 1993 Abingdon Press. Used by permission.

14 See "O the Depth of Love Divine," in *The United Methodist Hymnal* (Nashville: The United Methodist Publishing House, 1989), 627.

15 From "What Is Man?" in *The Works of John Wesley,* Volume 4, edited by Albert C. Outler, page 26. © 1987 Abingdon Press. Used by permission.

16 From "For Believers Rejoicing," in *The Works of John Wesley,* Volume 7, edited by Franz Hildebrandt and Oliver A. Beckerlegge, with the assistance of James Dale, pages 317–18. © 1983 Abingdon Press. Used by permission.

Chapter 4

Living With Others

*A*ccording to a recent poll, at least seven out of ten people among your friends, coworkers, and motorists passing you in their vehicles on the freeway say they believe in God. That is a significant increase in just the last decade (up eleven percent). Half of those people also say prayer is important in their daily life, and more than half believe in miracles as manifestations of the power of God. Some attribute this rise in faith to a popular wave of interest in angels and in television shows that feature spiritual values. At the same time, police struggle to gain control of illegal drug use, deadbeat dads, and road rage. We are torn by illegal militia activities, the threat of domestic terrorism, threatening nations abroad, and the rising number of juvenile felonies. While current data indicates that violent crime seems to be on the decrease, we feel more exposed to such crime because of its random nature and the blaring ways in which the media headline such offenses.

In this mix of faith and unfaith, we Christians are called to live out the meaning of Christ's teachings. We are not always clear, however, just how to live Christ's way in such a conflicted world. Many of our politicians say they are religious people, but there seems to be a feeling among them that Christ's teaching on turning the other cheek, for example, will not work in the tough world of politics and international relations. Some imply that while Jesus is good for the individual, the ways of Jesus are not good for the nation and the world. But the Wesleys did not believe this. They believed that if the love of God is turned loose on the world, it can impact everything. We need not check our Bibles at the door of our businesses, political arenas, negotiations, or whatever. John Wesley goes so far as to say that there is no holiness except social holiness. If holiness (the way of Christ) cannot work in the world, it simply cannot work. The gospel can be strong medicine for nations founded on greed, power, and provincialism; it can tear them down. Ancient Rome is a mute witness to that. Perhaps in no place is the disturbing message of the gospel more demanding than in the political world.

The Sermon on the Mount (Matthew 5–7), which contains the heart of Jesus' ethic of the Kingdom, is a political statement, a directory for the life of the *polis* (Jesus' "people"). In this sermon, Jesus speaks to the hard issues of interpersonal relationships, violent people we have to deal with, and the risk of peacemaking. John Wesley wrote thirteen sermons on the Sermon on the Mount. He believed that these sayings of the Lord are not just nice advice for the past but challenging goals for our life in the world. The Sermon on the Mount, particularly the Beatitudes (Matthew 5:3-12), made this sermon's first hearers gasp. It was—and still is—a gauntlet thrown down. In the previous chapter, we studied Wesley's view of spiritual growth, which he called works of piety. Now we will look at the Wesleys' concern for Christian life in the world, which John Wesley called "works of mercy."[1] The previous chapters and this one will lay the foundation for Wesley's most distinctive teaching: the doctrine of "Christian perfection" or "holiness of heart." We will take up that fantastic subject in the chapter to come.

The Royal Way

Once again we see John Wesley's high view of Jesus when we read in Wesley's writing that the complete will of God is displayed in the Lord's Sermon on the Mount. This is the "royal way" that leads us to the Kingdom. If we take a look at the sermon, we will gain some perspective on what it means to live as "altogether a Christian."[2] Matthew reports that Jesus and a crowd of people, including the disciples, were on a mountainside and that the Lord sat down and taught everyone as follows:

> Blessed are the poor in spirit, for theirs is the kingdom of heaven.
> Blessed are those who mourn, for they will be comforted.
> Blessed are the meek, for they will inherit the earth.
> Blessed are those who hunger and thirst for righteousness,
> for they will be filled.
> Blessed are the merciful, for they will receive mercy.
> Blessed are the pure in heart, for they will see God.
> Blessed are the peacemakers, for they will be called
> children of God.
> Blessed are those who are persecuted for righteousness' sake, for
> theirs is the kingdom of heaven.   (Matthew 5:3-10)

Of these beatitudes, four have to do principally with our inward life, and four deal principally with our relationships with others. The Jews who were present the day Jesus spoke would have heard him say that those who are broken in spirit ("the poor in spirit"), who realize their deep need of God, will inherit the kingdom of God. Wesley was right in saying that these people know themselves (as convicted of sin) and turn to God for forgiveness. Wesley saw this as the first step toward the Kingdom. The second beatitude has to do with mourning. Matthew tells us that the crowd that came to hear the Lord contained many people who were sick, physically and emotionally. Undoubtedly, they "mourned" their condition, but this is not what the Lord means. Jesus is referring to those awakened to God and who now are in sorrow over their sins and the sins of their neighbors. They mourn having disobeyed God. Wesley points out that this second beatitude reflects the seriousness with which we should think of our lives.

The third beatitude, on the meek, refers not to those who are physically weak or retiring in their personalities, but to those who do not insist on having their own way. This is important in the light of the first two beatitudes and means that these people should listen to what God wants, rather than doing what they might think is best. Sometimes *meek* is translated as *gentle*. Our Lord may have had Psalm 37:11 in mind when he said that such people "inherit the earth." In the fourth beatitude, which completes the attitude of the person determined to please God, Jesus speaks about being hungry and thirsty for righteousness. These are people who actively seek spiritual nourishment.

These four beatitudes lead us naturally to our relationships with others, which is the main concern of this chapter. In Christ, we want more than anything else to live according to God's will. As Christians, we want to be just and kind in all we do; we yearn to do right. The promise is that we will be "filled" (satisfied). To be satisfied does not mean that we have reached the limits of grace. "This thirst," Wesley claims, "shall endure for ever."[3] Actually, this profile of a follower of Jesus helps us understand the rugged character of the life we are to live.

The Horizontal Look

Know yourself, take sin seriously, listen only to God, seek God with your whole heart—these are the principles that guide our devotion. They are also the foundation for the horizontal dimensions of our life, as we will see. Now we turn to the four social beatitudes.

Happy are the merciful. In his small commentary on the New Testament, John Wesley translates *blessed* as *happy,* which is a good word to use. He could also have used the words *fully satisfied. Happiness* here is that deep sense of oneness with God, a oneness that produces a sense of peace, spiritual rest, feelings of being accepted. I am going to use the word *happy,* but we must keep in mind that we are not using it in any shallow, slaphappy sense.

Mercy is one of the main words of our faith. It is much more than a sentiment; it is an action. Mercy can be seen. Wherever we seek understanding, wherever we are willing to give the benefit of the doubt, wherever we help someone without thought of getting something in return, we are acting with mercy. Mercy is not pity; mercy is active "charity," as Wesley puts it. Mercy is more than good will; it is a willingness to forgive. Mercy is at its height when it is given to those who deserve it least. This does not mean bypassing justice, but it does mean being tenderhearted. In my state, a teen filled with anger shot into a group of Christian youth at school, killing several and wounding others. Although devastated by grief, the parents of one of the girls who was killed spoke of their daughter's killer with mercy, not hatred. They then donated their daughter's internal organs so that others might live. They were in every way examples of mercy. In the interests of justice, however, the boy must accept the consequences of his action. Even when we are forgiven by God, the results of our sins often have a terrible aftermath.

John Wesley interprets this beatitude on extending mercy by using Paul's teaching on love in 1 Corinthians 13:4-7:

> Love is patient; love is kind; love is not envious or boastful or arrogant or rude. It does not insist on its own way; it is not irritable or resentful; it does not rejoice in wrongdoing, but rejoices in the truth. It bears all things, believes all things, hopes all things, endures all things.

Phrase by phrase, Wesley expounds Paul's view of love. Wesley speaks of a Christian life that is pleased with the accomplishments of others and that is kind to all people. Such a person neither jumps to conclusions nor assumes that his or her judgments are always right. A Christian wants good relationships with others, at least insofar as it is possible for us to promote. Following Jesus, we replace jealousy with appreciation, falsehood with truth. Wesley believed that Christians can absorb a lot of shock, as the family of the slain teenager did, and still believe in God's goodness. That goodness is possible in our daily lives. Wesley interprets Paul's words in social terms. This is Christian behavior motivated by love, energized by the desire to please God, and desirous of the best for others. In effect, love is wanting for others what you want for yourself and working for that to happen. Mercy can be understood as love expressed.

The promise for extending mercy is that we will receive mercy (from God). God accepts those who accept others, who work for the improvement of their lives when they can. Mercy is what we need, as well as what we need to give. We are not so perfect that we do not need understanding and forgiveness. Even the saintly Francis of Assisi, famous for his humility and generosity, considered himself a sinner in need of God's mercy. Francis was right. Think what your home, your workplace, the town or city in which you live would be like if mercy were freely given and sincerely received. Our prisons would surely be less full. What we strive for is to model for others the mercy we have received from God.

Happy are the pure in heart. This language of purity of heart seems strange to us. What does it mean to be pure in heart in our social and family relationships? Wesley says it means to see God in all things, which is a good way to put it. Mother Teresa was a splendid example of this beatitude. She saw Christ in the faces of the dying poor. Each one was a representation of the Lord, and she cared for them as she wanted to care for Christ.

Dietrich Bonhoeffer was a Lutheran minister and teacher who lived during the years of World War II. He was popular at the time and wrote many books on living as a Christian. He was captured by the Nazis and later hanged by them just before his prison camp was liberated by the Allies. Bonhoeffer, in his book *Life Together,* gives an example of what Wesley means by purity of heart: Whenever two Christians meet and exchange greetings, there is an occasion of Christ meeting Christ. That thought revolutionized my life as a young pastor. I would stand in the foyer greeting people after worship and see in them and their remarks reflections of Christ for me. It was wonderful! I hope they saw in my remarks (some as casual as "Good morning") Christ's grace extended to them.

Wesley said nature itself bears eloquent testimony to the reality and power of God. Here, Wesley reminds me of the writings of the Jewish essayist Isaac Bashevis Singer, who died some years ago. Singer was an optimist most of his life and spoke of God as an artist, painting hope and love in nature and history. Singer was aware of great evil in the world, and he knew how much his people suffered at the hands of Adolf Hitler and those like him. Some of Singer's best short stories came out of the experiences of Jews in Poland before and during World War II. Yet even these hardships did not completely erase his hopes in God's control over the affairs of the world. Singer's short stories tell about triumph in the midst of the complexities of life. Like Singer, Wesley saw great evil unleashed in human society, but he was also able to see God's goodness. Part of the greatness of being human is knowing that the sun rises after the dark of night. But if we cannot see the dawn, at least we can hope for it and to that extent, at a minimum, can put some goodness back into life.

Purity of heart would have been understood by biblical writers as a mind tightly focused on God's will. To desire to please God is to be pure in heart, since the heart has only one basic goal. To me, this beatitude of Jesus has enormous possibilities for race relations in America. To be pure in heart would be to look at other people and see God, not different colors or languages or social customs. This is obviously the way Jesus looked at others. The promise attached to this beatitude by the Lord is that such people will see God. Surely Jesus means seeing God in others, but there is more. Seeing God now, therefore, has an eternal dimension to it. But the vision of God in heaven—that is, the seeing of the glory of God in its fullness in God's kingdom—is the height of happiness, in Wesley's understanding.

Happy are the peacemakers. The Beatitudes seem to progress in importance for Wesley; each one takes us a little deeper into the ethic of the Kingdom. Those who are merciful to others and see God in others are busy about making peace. Right here we face the evil of the world head on. Have you noticed that the Bible does not define evil; rather, it is satisfied to describe instances of it. One of the most common experiences of evil is in the hostility people often feel toward one another. The author of Psalm 120 complains that he has lived too long "among those who hate peace." He groans: "I am for peace; but when I speak, they are for war" (6-7). It is better for people to live in peace, and it is especially good when the family is at peace (Psalm 133).

Our world has known little peace throughout its history. In the thirty-five centuries of recorded history, there have been only 268 years of universal peace.[4] Hopes for peace today are complicated by the possibility of rogue nations creating and using nuclear and chemical or biological agents of mass destruction. What we have seen on the major news networks lately adds freshness to Charles Wesley's sentiments in one of his hymns:

> Prince of universal peace,
>> Destroy the enmity;
> Bid our jars and discords cease,
>> Unite us all in thee!
> Cruel as wild beasts we are
> Till vanquished by thy mercy's power,
> Men like wolves each other tear,
>> And their own flesh devour.[5]

No wonder in the same hymn Wesley considers men as "human savages." One wonders if Wesley is fair to the "wolves" and "leopards," since their killer instinct is just that, instinct. Humans are killers by choice, as an act of the will. To respond by saying that Wesley accepts a just-war theory is to miss his point. Ragged violent aggression wells up from the depths of the human heart. The cause may be fear, a lack of ego-strength in leaders, a pathology of being divinely chosen to conquer, or whatever. The cure, Wesley constantly reminds us, is not the power of art or philosophy or education, or the renovation of cities or providing clean air, or even greater military might, as wonderful as these things might be. The cure is a heart made free of the need to hurt, made free by the gospel of Jesus Christ. Who offers that? The Peacemaker.

Wesley chastised the church for its complicity in causing pain, subduing people, and creating havoc, which made a bad social situation worse. The intention of the Wesley brothers was to "reform the nation, particularly the Church; and to spread scriptural holiness over the land."[6] Especially the church because the church was lax on such social issues as slavery and the brutal treatment of children. John Wesley (the reformer), like the ancient prophet, had courage to tell the truth and to attempt to bring about social change. The church must be careful because, though redeemed, it can make a choice to brutalize, reduce dignity, and enslave others to its own rules. The Ten Commandments (Exodus 20:1-17) are designed to maximize freedom, fidelity, and security and to minimize the risk, always real, that the people of God will usurp divine authority for their own ends. To be fair, some clergy and laity in the established Church of England during Wesley's time wanted righteousness to prevail, but there were too few of them to change much. The point here is not for us to bash the church every opportunity we have, but to challenge the church to stand by its convictions and be Christ's witness without compromising the gospel.

Wesley urges us to confront evil with good and to do good to all people when and how we can. We are not to be frightened by the complexity of the problems we face; we are to witness to the Savior, who alone can so change the human heart that blessing and not cursing follows. The promise of this beatitude is that we will be called "children of God." If to love and promote peace is to be a child of God, then God must desire peace and love on the face of the earth. Like parent, like child, especially here in that God loves and creates life, not death. Christ conquers death by his death and resurrection. The power with which we witness is not our own, but rather that of the resurrected Lord through the Spirit of Pentecost, that Spirit who can help us communicate with others in ideas and images they can understand.

Reflecting on the beatitudes mentioned thus far, Wesley concludes that any person attempting to live as the Beatitudes direct should be the "darling" of humanity. Unfortunately, such is not the case. So Wesley turns to the last of the beatitudes, the last aspect of the character of those who would follow Christ. It is a daring and difficult beatitude.

Happy are those who are persecuted for righteousness' sake. To characterize people as happy who are undergoing persecution shows us the truly unique quality of gospel happiness. It is anything but happiness produced by comfort and security, which is what we usually think of when we think of a happy and good life. In fact, many people whom we once may have thought had it made have lived miserable and even meaningless lives. Being privileged is no guarantee of blessedness. But neither is being poor, although the gospel message considers poor people the special subject of God's message of the Kingdom. What matters is faithfulness, which this last beatitude underscores. And to keep us from missing the point, Jesus restates it even more strongly in verse 11. In this verse, our Lord describes persecution as being reviled (hated, condemned, defamed) and even being falsely accused of various crimes. To say one is happy under such circumstances seems puzzling indeed.

Why should Christians be hated in the first place? Here, Wesley was as mystified as the rest of us. Wesley, in his sermon "Upon Our Lord's Sermon on the Mount, XII," comments on false prophets (preachers): "The way to heaven…is the way of lowliness, mourning, meekness, and holy desire, love of God and of our neighbor, doing good, and suffering evil for Christ's sake."[7] These beatitudes are characteristics of those who want to improve themselves and the lives of others. Such people announce the will of God and try to live it themselves. These are the people who would do good to others, show no cause for anger, and willingly share what they have so that all may have something. Wesley is describing your life in Christ, a life of self-giving in response to Christ's self-giving. Why should someone hate you for this?

Nowhere is the paradox of our faith in the world more starkly stated than it is here. We are not the darlings of society. The church of the apostles understood that being persecuted is for the sake of Christ and his teachings (Acts 5:17-42). This persecution is serious. Simply because one is not liked does not mean one is persecuted in the Gospel sense. Gospel persecution is tied to witnessing to one's faith. I have known Christians who thought they were being persecuted for their faith when they were being shunned because of their bad attitude, because of their judgmental spirit, or because they were obnoxious to be around. Gospel persecution is fundamentally caused by people's attitude toward Jesus.

Charles Wesley wrote a poem titled "Written in D[ubli]n," which he likely wrote in response to a mob he faced in Ireland, probably in 1747–48. The Methodists often felt the heat of mob rule. Stanza 5, which is the last, catches the tone of the whole poem:

> An Outcast for my Master's sake
>   Haste, ye Ruffian Band, to take
>   This mournful Life of mine;
> A Life by Sin & Sorrow stain'd,
> A Life, which I have long disdain'd,
>   And languish'd to resign.[8]

There is "no Justice...for Christians here," Charles Wesley writes in Stanza 4. Respect would come eventually for the Wesleys, but not for another twenty years or so. Considered fanatics by many people, the Wesleys and other Methodists had to bear the howl and scorn—and occasionally the violence—of the masses. To their credit, I can find no instance where the Wesleys pressed charges against their tormentors. We would do well while sitting in the comfort and safety of our pews to remember the price once paid for our privileges.

The promise for this beatitude is the same as for the first beatitude: "Theirs is the kingdom of heaven." Now we have come full circle. The first beatitude speaks of our poverty before God, the last of our poverty before our enemies. In between is a progression of spiritual life, moving from a cultivation of love for God to an outpouring of love for others. The remainder of the Sermon on the Mount illustrates these principles of spiritual life. For the Wesleys, what we do for others in some way relates to these teachings of Jesus. Christians do not need a large book of rules for living, only the Beatitudes as taught by the Lord. But the Beatitudes need to be rightly understood. Of course, we will be judged by these same principles. Christians are not armchair quarterbacks; we are in the game itself, and the stakes are eternal.

"Saved to Serve"

In the General Rules of the Methodist Societies, John Wesley provided a summary of Christian behavior, which he expected to be read regularly to Methodist congregations. These rules, with specific examples under each, fall under three headings: "Avoid all the evil you can," "Do all the good you can," and "Attend the means of grace." The Wesleys were concerned with self-help, self-protection, and self-giving. The fact that Wesley could condense Christian ethics to three general axioms is remarkable. The last one, "Attend the means of grace," is the fuel that enables one to do good and avoid evil. Perhaps this axiom really ought to be placed first in the list. Nonetheless, Wesley expects us, as Methodists, to let God feed our souls and inspire us to a better life, a deeper life, a more responsible life. By saying we should do all we can is to recognize that our best efforts may be rejected and our best intentions misunderstood. This does not stop us; rather, such resistance merely widens the scope of our life to include the Beatitudes we have been studying in this chapter.

Naturally, our early brothers and sisters faced constant risk because one cannot continually be confronted by non-Christian, secular values and not be tempted to make them one's own. The same is true for us. As I have mentioned above, we do not live in a society consciously shaped by Christian faith any more than the Wesleys did. Secular people are hesitant to allow religious values to influence education, sexual ethics, and international politics. At the same time, we recently have seen the value of prayer in healing after surgery, a resurgence of "family values" (largely Christian), and pro football teams kneeling in prayer over a seriously injured player on the field.

Borrowing a phrase from The Salvation Army, an offshoot of the Wesleyan Revival, we are "saved to serve." The personal yearning for God seen in the first four beatitudes naturally flows into the action for others seen in the last four beatitudes. Even if the consequences for us are negative, we still work for good in the world, and thereby follow the path of the incarnating God (God for us, in us, through us). We are never amazed at seeing Christians working in soup kitchens, in halfway houses, in places of refuge for abused people, as counselors on hotlines, as care givers to marginalized children, as volunteers in hospitals here and abroad, as people praying for social change. In his sermon "On Visiting the Sick," John Wesley says: "The walking herein [in 'good works,' Ephesians 2:10] is essentially necessary...to the continuance of that faith whereby we 'are' already 'saved by grace'...to the attainment of everlasting salvation."[9] Do you get the importance of this? Good works of mercy are the sure sign of vital faith. This is our Christian duty, not of drudgery but of joy and with thanksgiving.

This is holiness shown. By living deeply, we live outwardly. This is love turned loose, and who can tell the end of it? Nowhere is Wesleyan optimism more noticeable than here in the belief—no, the absolute conviction—that love can reign. In spite of the seemingly insurmountable odds of such love really happening, this dream of a people loving God and one another drove the Wesleys night and day. Without regard to defections from the revival, troublesome preachers, harassing from hecklers, and plain old bodily weariness, the Wesleys (especially John) traveled the British Isles "[spreading] scriptural holiness over the land" for the sole purpose of enhancing life for those who would hear and believe. What better heritage can we have than this? A heritage solidly anchored in the "plain" teachings of Scripture, shaped by the desire to please God, and unselfconsciously giving to others—this is the flag under which we march. Such is living our common faith deeply and to the fullest possible.

Concluding Thoughts

One of the most important teachings of Christian faith is the Incarnation of Jesus. This means that the divinity of God was coupled with the humanity of Jesus to produce a totally unique person. The early church believed that Jesus was God in the flesh, and that this fact has enormous implications for humanity. This means at the very least that God creates humans, loves humans, and identifies with humans. Nothing that concerns you and me is minor to God. What you think, value, and do is tremendously important to God. God wants to be involved in your life to the fullest. I heard a colleague of mine preach in our chapel the great truth that "God loves every one of us as though there were but one of us to love."

The love inside us spills over to those around us. This is the Christian life. In the previous chapter and in this one, we have looked at Wesley's teaching on holy love within and holy love acting on the world. In the next chapter, we will look more closely at exactly what the Wesleys mean by holiness. We will discover there the heart of our faith: God has called us to be filled with Christ and to live Christ's way.

Probing Our Faith

1. If you were to really live deeply your life in Christ, what would that mean in how you relate to people you know?
2. What issues in our society ought to be of concern to the church? How, do you think, can the church speak to these issues? What can you do?
3. Read Jesus' warning to his disciples in Matthew 24:9-14. What, do you think, did those disciples feel when they heard what Jesus had to say? What if Jesus were to say the same thing to you?
4. John Wesley preached more about the power, influence, and right use of money than any other ethical topic. Why would he do this to a society composed basically of haves and have-nots? What might Wesley say to Wall Street today? What might he say to us?

ENDNOTES

1 From "Upon Our Lord's Sermon on the Mount, VI," in *The Works of John Wesley*, Volume 1, edited by Albert C. Outler, page 573. © 1984 Abingdon Press. Used by permission.

2 From "The Almost Christian," in *The Works of John Wesley*, Volume 1, edited by Albert C. Outler, page 131. © 1984 Abingdon Press. Used by permission.

3 From "Upon Our Lord's Sermon on the Mount, II," in *The Works of John Wesley*, Volume 1, edited by Albert C. Outler, page 497. © 1984 Abingdon Press. Used by permission.

4 See *The Lessons of History*, by Will and Ariel Durant (New York: Simon and Schuster, 1968), page 81.

5 From "For Believers Interceding for the World," in *The Works of John Wesley*, Volume 7, edited by Franz Hildebrandt and Oliver A. Beckerlegge, with the assistance of James Dale, page 612. © 1983 Abingdon Press. Used by permission.

6 From "Minutes of Several Conversations Between the Rev. Mr. Wesley and Others, From the Year 1744 to the Year 1789," in *The Works of John Wesley*, Volume VIII (Grand Rapids: Zondervan Publishing House, 1872 reprint), page 299.

7 From "Upon Our Lord's Sermon on the Mount, XII," in *The Works of John Wesley*, Volume 1, edited by Albert C. Outler, page 677. © 1984 Abingdon Press. Used by permission.

8 From "Written in D[ubli]n," in *The Unpublished Poetry of Charles Wesley: Hymns and Poems for Church and World*, Volume III, edited by S. T. Kimbrough, Jr., and Oliver A. Beckerlegge, page 129. © 1992 Abingdon Press. Used by permission.

9 From "On Visiting the Sick," in *The Works of John Wesley*, Volume 3, edited by Albert C. Outler, pages 385–86. © 1986 Abingdon Press. Used by permission.

Chapter 5

God's Will Alone, My One Desire

*T*he human spirit always cries out for more, especially once it has been touched by the divine. When we have been touched by the divine, we look up from the tide pool and move toward the ocean! The quest is not for more goods or more power or even more life, for the time comes when all of that is worthless. We cry out for more understanding, more hope, more love, more of God. In recounting the sorry history of Israel, the prophet Isaiah bemoaned the people's fate. Jerusalem was crushed, the beautiful Temple was destroyed, and God was silent. Yet in the midst of his prayer for God's anger to be turned aside, this confused Jewish seer confesses what only believers can confess, even during times of blood and fire: "O Lord, you are our Father; we are the clay, and you are our potter; we are all the work of your hand" (Isaiah 64:8). These words of pathos and humility are cries for God to remake the people and to do so in the way God wants. In that moment of darkness, Isaiah (son of Amoz) was a holy man. He prayed as only a holy person can pray.

This desire to have God remake life compelled John and Charles Wesley to turn to the teachings of the sages as though they were the fountain of youth. Captivated by the desire that drove men and women of the fourth century of the Common Era into the scorching deserts in search of God, that moved merchants to become monks, and that changed women like Mary of Egypt from flagrant (and high-class) prostitution to the life of a woman known for her devotion to God, John Wesley (like them) wanted God. In our increasingly secular culture, you and I have difficulty grasping this kind of magnificent obsession to know and love God. Yet, my reader, this obsession is in your heart or else you would not have read so far in this book. This quest is still alive for you, and it is still alive in the hearts of women and men I know who work in ghettos, in jungles, in classrooms, in offices. It is all for the love of God, to know God, and to do God's will. They live the psalmist's prayer:

> O God, you are my God, I seek you,
>   my soul thirsts for you;
> my flesh faints for you,
>   as in a dry and weary land
>   where there is no water.
>   (Psalm 63:1)

To this point in our work together, we have taken a close look at the God who loves us (Chapter 1) and the enemies who would bring us down (Chapter 2). In the light of this glory and temptation, we have looked at the Wesleys' concern for personal relationship with God (Chapter 3) and social responsibility (Chapter 4). I have deliberately waited until now to try to put in some perspective the doctrine of "holiness of heart and life"[1] that flows out of the first four chapters. This chapter is the heart of the mystery of grace for the Wesleys: the willingness of the almighty God to touch human life and put God's likeness there. This chapter will lead us to the next one, where we will look at two important aspects of our new life in Christ: the assurance of God's saving grace and the church as the nurturing fellowship for Christian life.

The Depths of Grace

Wesley saw the depths of grace most clearly in the teachings of Jesus, especially in the Gospel of John and in the three letters of John (1, 2, and 3 John). One of the best-loved portions of John's gospel are the words our Lord spoke during a heated argument between some Pharisees and Sadducees. This exchange will help us grasp the scope of holiness of life. At one point in the give-and-take, a lawyer asks Jesus to tell them which is the greatest commandment. Combining Deuteronomy 6:5 and Leviticus 19:18, Jesus says:

> "You shall love the Lord your God with all your heart, and with all your soul, and with all your mind." This is the greatest and first commandment. And a second is like it: "You shall love your neighbor as yourself." On these two commandments hang all the law and the prophets. (Matthew 22:37-40)

In his own spiritual classic, "A Plain Account of Christian Perfection," John Wesley coupled this teaching on love of God and neighbor with love of enemies. In the Sermon on the Mount, you may recall, Jesus talks about how we are to respond to those who abuse us: "Be perfect, therefore, as your heavenly Father is perfect" (Matthew 5:48). In this short sentence, we see the basis for Wesley's understanding of Christian perfection: unselfish love motivating one's heart.[2]

The word *pure*, for Wesley, meant unmixed. For example, pure love for God would be love without a rival. Pure love for your neighbor would be the sincere desire to do your neighbor all the good you could possibly do. Pure love for one's enemies would be a yearning for them to turn from their evil ways and be genuinely converted to God. This yearning includes our doing what we can to help this happen, if we can do anything at all. If we cannot do anything, then we yearn for someone else to help our enemy. A converted enemy is much better than a vicious one. But pure love for an enemy also means a serious look at ourselves to determine if we are that person's enemy and if we are yearning for their conversion to make us look better. Praying for our enemies demands humility and genuine self-searching.

Some suggest that the word *unrestricted* is the best way to understand Jesus' saying that we should love our enemies as God loves them. So how does God love them? God provides them with opportunities to change and to amend their ways, and encourages them to do so. We can do no less. This is an honest effort, not one with an undercurrent of anger or of seeking revenge. Such love may be rejected—as God's love is at times—but that is something we cannot control. We do what we can with a heart to do good. Thus, love for God, neighbor, and enemy is a matter of behavior as well as of attitude.

We can easily say that we love God or that we love a good neighbor. Although we may not want to admit the fact, it is actually the enemy that is the true measure of our commitment to righteous living. Luke also records in his gospel Jesus' words about loving our enemies. I must say his teaching was as startling to his hearers as it is to us. In Jesus' day, most people believed that one ought to harm enemies, not help them. We often think the same way. But Jesus unmistakably says that true followers of God have an active, open concern for the welfare of their enemy. We want the enemy to stop doing wrong and do right. So, when we can, we are to do everything in our power to do good to those who openly do bad. Such desire on a Christian's part does not mitigate the enemy's responsibility for evil done, nor does it set aside a just sentence in a court of law. But it is the intentional focusing of one's self upon God, the intentional working for the neighbor's good, and even attempting to do good for those who are counted as enemies. This, Jesus says, is being like God. God loves bad people not because they are bad but because they can become good.

This idea can cause problems for some of us, myself included. I understand these difficulties when terrible evil hits home. We experience a mixture of shock, anger, confusion, and perhaps vengeance. When evil slaps you in the face and chaos consumes everything dear to you, you are sent reeling. I have been there, and all these feelings are real. But the crucified Jesus can give crucified people a hope of resurrection. And only the power of God can enable us to want peace instead of vengeance, to want hope instead of revenge, and to act with restraint instead of malice. The lasting fate of the enemy is God's business.

The crown of God's grace, made possible by God's own self-giving (especially on the cross), is for us to do for others without expecting anything back, to act righteously even when we know for sure the only thing coming back to us is scorn and contempt. Such love is really perfect and unmixed—that is, it includes no thought of payback. Clearly, this love is tough, not mushy. Such love demands justice; yet it is still love. Purity of heart is measured against a standard outside ourselves—that is, in keeping with the conviction that holiness is centered only in God's just power to create, sustain, and order the world.

John Wesley also turned to the letter of 1 John for his understanding of Christian perfection. John the Beloved lived when the Christian community was being ripped apart by division and threatened with persecution. His letter was an attempt to help Christians recognize what was happening and what to do about it:

> Whoever says, "I have come to know [God]," but does not obey his commandments, is a liar, and in such a person the truth does not exist; but whoever obeys his word, truly in this person the love of God has reached perfection.   (1 John 2:4-5a)

This is an echo of the Old Testament: Love of God consists in doing what God says. Our obedience to God is at the same time our yes to holiness of life. We need to keep in mind, though, that for Old Testament believers, the law of Moses determined what God wanted; in the New Testament, it is Jesus who is the standard. "Little children," John writes, "let us love, not in word or speech, but in truth and action" (1 John 3:18). Given to Jesus, we have, as Paul says, the "mind" of Christ (Philippians 2:5), which is humbly obedient to the will of God and full of trust in God.

The question for Wesley seems to be, Can we give ourselves so fully to God that God's will shapes what we think, say, and do? Do the biblical writers tease us, so to speak, with a life that is totally beyond us? Or to put it another way, Can we respond to life in an unselfconscious way, motivated only by the love of God in Jesus Christ? For Wesley, the answer to this question is an unqualified yes.

What Is Our Problem?

The history of Christian spirituality is filled with writings on how to mature in the Christian life. Wesley was familiar with that history, and what he read spoke to his heart. In the early sermon "The Circumcision of the Heart" (1733), Wesley concludes by saying that we should desire nothing but to praise God's name. That is, live every day with the firm intention to think and do what will please God. By *intention* Wesley means we should have a "steadfast regard"[3] (or a real desire) for God's glory in all we do. Wesley did not intend to lay out an impossible ideal for us. Far from it! This is a practical matter. Jesus came in order to help us turn from the chaos in our lives to the order in God's life, from the negative feelings we sometimes have to the joy of the Lord, from a mind filled with bad thoughts and ideas to a mind focused only on God and God's goodness. Wesley saw this teaching in both the Bible and the writings of the saints.

Taken seriously, such thoughts light up as fire in our hearts. Wesley says we can live a life of praise to God; we can allow God to work in us fully; we can firmly intend to manifest God's glory in all we do. This is practical advice. And by God's grace, we can live just such a life. Why, then, aren't most Christians living this way? Wesley says that even Christians do battle with disobedience, which is another way of saying *sin*.

But have we not confessed our sins, been baptized in the strong name of Jesus, and promised before the congregation that we will live according to the teachings of Scripture? Wesley says we have, and if we hold firm to that confession, we will enter the kingdom to come. By grace we have been changed. But, as the major denominations of Christian faith teach, a serious flaw still resides in us.

To help explain this, Wesley uses King David of the Old Testament as an example of what he means. David had new life in God, lived by faith in God's will, and loved God sincerely. One morning this revered leader and king saw Bathsheba, another man's wife, bathing. That was the beginning of temptation rising and the vision of God diminishing. "He loved God still," Wesley points out, "but not in the same degree."[4] The fall of this noble king demonstrated to Wesley that even deep and sincere faith can be shattered gradually and finally forsaken. David did not have to sin with this beautiful woman, but he chose to do so. None of us is dragged down by surprise but by our own consent. What we need is the instant inward resistance to evil from without, with no wavering within.

Charles Wesley put these sentiments into many hymns. In a section of the *Hymns* called "Groaning for Full Redemption," the early Methodists sang about their search for stability in faith. The following is one example:

> Let earth no more my heart divide;
> With Christ may I be crucified,
>   To thee with my whole soul aspire;
> Dead to the world and all its toys,
> Its idle pomp, and fading joys,
>   Be thou alone my one desire.[5]

We see here what many sense, that overcoming evil has many dimensions. Today, with the benefits of psychoanalysis, we understand better how complicated the influences of our past are on our values and goals. The innocence we all hope can be restored seems to allude us, no matter how determined we are. Yet the Wesleys come with words of hope that the God who draws us to the very side of God will save us, even from ourselves.

"The Usual Course"

John Wesley believed that the Sermon on the Mount is meant for our lives in the here and now. It charts our normal course. Some say that is expecting too much, that the Sermon on the Mount cannot really be lived until we enter heaven. Who is right? What does the Lord expect from us? Without question, God expects total commitment. But total commitment does not mean we have a fully matured spiritual life at once. Rather, total commitment means we are set firmly on a course to get everything God wants to give us. (And what God wants to give us may vary from person to person.) I was reading a book of spiritual teaching by a missionary writer that said something like this: To never thirst (for God), one must ever thirst. That is really true. Neither Wesley would dare suggest that struggles are ever over for the Christian, or that we can flippantly dismiss the temptations that come our way.

Charles Wesley is especially careful about rushing spiritual development. Because of the many somewhat-weird spiritual manifestations among early Methodists, Charles wrote an especially

powerful poem about claiming too much too soon. He was
inspired to write this poem while reading Matthew 9:17 ("Neither
is new wine put into old wineskins; otherwise, the skins burst, and
the wine is spilled, and the skins are destroyed"). The poem has
five stanzas. We will look at selected lines only.

1. We run before the grace divine,
2.   If, while their hearts are unrenew'd,
3. Hard tasks we rig'rously injoin,
4.   And yokes impose on converts rude...
5. While warm with undiscerning zeal,
6.   We urge the novice on too fast,
7. To scale at once the holiest hill,
8.   As his first labour were his last:
9. He swells as wholly sanctified,
10.   As perfect in a moment's space,
11. He bursts with self-important pride,
12.   And loses all his real grace....
13. Our only wisdom is, to trace
14.   The path whereby the Spirit leads,
15. The usual course of saving grace,
16.   Which step by step in souls proceeds.[6]

Lines 1–8 tell us that sometimes we push people too hard and
want them to make spiritual progress too fast. I have seen this
many times when a new convert was made the teacher of a Sunday
school class or a leader in the church before she or he could really
handle that kind of assignment. Lines 9–12 point out the danger
this causes when it produces pride instead of humility. The idea
that one could lose "real grace" in this process is frightening. Lines
13–16 point us to wisdom, to "the usual course" that leads us into
God "step by step." The Psalms tend to emphasize the idea of
waiting before God. Sometimes we wait because we have no other
choice, but at other times waiting inspires us to grow in God.
Charles Wesley displayed much wisdom here. This does not mean
we should be slack in pursuing God; Wesley says quite the oppo-
site. What Charles Wesley does through this poem is save us from
saying things about ourselves that our lives do not back up.

However, we must allow at least that God knows best how we
are to proceed in the way of faith. If slowly, fine; if rapidly, fine.

We have no special interest here, only that our lives have God as their center, and that we remember that Jesus was the world's only perfect person.

Simplicity of Life

William Law was a contemporary of John and Charles Wesley and highly respected as a writer on spiritual life. His works, particularly his second book, *A Serious Call to a Devout and Holy Life,* were important in the development of John Wesley's view of evangelical perfection (in love). Perhaps Law's most important contribution to the Wesleys was his teaching on "singleness of intention." This is an easy concept to grasp and is one that seems immediately obvious—namely, God is to have preeminence in our life, and our single objective in life is to please God. Law teaches that the only rule for our life is to live for Christ, who died and rose from the dead in order that we might be redeemed. Law is unconcerned whether one is a politician, a newscaster, a truck driver, or a home builder; all of us are required to bring our lives in line with the will of God as we see that will revealed in Christ.

Following Law, Wesley concluded that both wisdom and Scripture teach us to narrow our focus to only one working principle or rule: to aim for the glory of God in all we think, say, and do. Probably the first sermon the young John Wesley preached in America was "A Single Intention," an idea that shows up in his small tract *The Character of a Methodist.*

Biographers of Law and Wesley point out that both were serious young men, which means that they were probably as unusual in their day as they would be in ours. They realized, as we do, that few people have an overriding value that shapes what they do. Both point out that Christians must beware of competing values for the love of God. When I was a teen, we used to encourage each other in our church youth group by saying we should be "sold out" to God. That was a teenager's way of saying what Wesley means.

When discussing the Wesleys' views on spiritual life, we need to remember two things: First, no matter how well-intentioned a person is, he or she will make mistakes. We have no way around that, since we are human and limited in intelligence, in ability to perform, and in clarity of thought. We can even do harm when we intend only to do good. This is not a matter of committing a sin, since sinning, for Wesley, involves a choice to do bad. The lesson here is, Do not expect more of yourself than is reasonable within your faith. You and I are humans. We can be hurt, disappointed, discouraged, even worried and still not sin against God.

Second, there is absolutely nothing you can do to earn God's favor. That favor is freely given because God is love. God loves us simply because we are, not because we produce something. We are Christians not because we want to go to heaven but because we want to please God. And how do we please God? By perfect performance? No. That is impossible. We please God by being lovingly obedient as God's human children to what we understand to be God's will at the time.

Wesley urged us to let our eye be "single" to the glory of God in our devotional life, our business practices, our recreation, our family life, and our conversations with others. But how do we cultivate a sensitivity to God in every aspect of our living? We do that by thinking about our lives, by integrating Scripture teaching into what we do, by praying about even the tiniest things, and by not hesitating to speak to God about everything. There is one other thing, too. We can talk about matters of faith with other people. I do not mean beating someone over the head with our faith. I mean sharing life and faith with someone who understands or who wants to understand. Wesley reminds us that in Christ "all things about [us have] become new"; therefore, walk in the freedom of that newness. "To love God, and to be beloved by [God], is enough."[7] That is true. Working, parenting, coping, helping, and sharing all flow from a single source: our hearts made new by the love of God. We are to live deeply and constantly our new life in Christ.

A Monument to God

Near the Potomac River in Arlington, Virginia, stands a monument to perfection. It is the United States Iwo Jima Memorial, which is a bronze monument showing six Marines trying to plant an American flag in battle-soaked soil. With weapons put aside and wholly exposed to enemy fire, they are poised to hoist Old Glory as a sacrificial act of heroism in the face of almost-certain death. The energy of that monument is electric and, no matter what one's view of war, one stands in amazement at men who would claim a scarred land for freedom. You see, the cause—not their individual moral or intellectual excellence—hallowed the men's intentions. Their heroism came from something greater than they were. Their act was one of defiance of an enemy force as much as it was of courage in doing what they would not ordinarily do. Whether in battle, in one's career, or simply in being a person, that monument stirs one to believe greatness is possible.

That monument is a human view of dedication. Theirs was a defining act, not simply for a half-dozen men but for a nation. That larger-than-life monument represents larger-than-life commitment, larger-than-life acting out. Now, this is one example of what holiness is: the focused determination that "come what may, I will live for a grand vision that is bigger than I am, even though it demands more than I can give." I do not know what each of those men felt the day their photograph was taken by a war correspondent, and I do not know what drove them to do a mighty act. But I do know that God calls us to heroic living in the face of suffering, and that by God's grace, it can be done.

Not everyone can raise a flag in the heat of battle; not everyone can do a deed so defining that it will be admired by generations. But everyone can carry a cross continually and deny what must be denied to bear the name of Christ. Everyone can follow Christ daily into that necessary struggle that shapes character and defines honor. It can be done because Christ says it can be done, and it can be done by you. Life can be formed and sustained by a grand vision of unquestioning allegiance. Such a life was lived by Francis of Assisi and Helen Keller, by Martin Luther King, Jr., and Mother Teresa. And just maybe by someone you know. The six men did what they did because it had to be done. They marshaled unknown courage; we give ourselves to the known Christ and his strength. Photographed or not, we can be energized by the great God and sustained by the Spirit to live the life required by our

Lord: total loving dedication to God's will and the good of others. Can it be done? We answered that at our baptism: With God's help, we can.

I first began studying John Wesley's views of Christian perfection nearly forty years ago. As a student pastor at that time, I read John Wesley's *A Plain Account of Christian Perfection* and then promptly laid it aside. The idea of perfection or purity of heart was so foreign to me that although I could easily embrace the whole of Wesleyan thought, I stumbled on the word *perfection*. After repeated study, not only of Wesley but of the larger tradition of the church, I have come to the place where I now embrace what I think he meant. Wesley did not put it as I am going to state it, but I honestly think he would have no difficulty with my interpretation of his thought. Purity of heart, or what Wesley calls "Christian perfection," is a clear and deep intuition that one is firmly rooted in God's love through Jesus Christ as the true condition of one's life. This means four things to me.

First, we can have an inner conviction—what I call a clear and deep intuition—that God is the absolute foundation for who we are and what we do. Who can explain this reality of an inner conviction so strong that we are willing to risk our lives for it? This conviction is something like what the apostle Paul described for Timothy: "I know the one in whom I have put my trust" (2 Timothy 1:12). Some things we know simply because we know them, not because we have been convinced of them by rational argument or even prior experience. This is a knowledge of the heart, and it is as firm as any knowledge of the head. As the psalmist reports in Psalm 125:1: "Those who trust in the LORD are like Mount Zion, which cannot be moved." They are firmly fixed.

Second, the content of this knowledge is that I am firmly rooted in God. This is to know oneself, the very thing we seem least likely to know. The saints whom I have read about are all in agreement on one thing: By God's grace, we can so commit ourselves to God that we take lasting delight in that relationship. This does not mean that life suddenly becomes easy or understandable. Life is a mystery laced with turmoil, but in the living of it we can know for sure that God is our anchor and our abiding light.

Third, what the heart knows is God through Jesus Christ in the power of the Holy Spirit. This is why I began this book with a discussion of God. What we know of God comes by God's own self-revelation. God is gracious and lets us in on just enough of the secret of divinity that we can rest in the midst of the storm. I love to read theological books, but Christian life is not about theology. Christian life is about God in us, "the hope of glory" (Colossians 1:27). God lets us in, through a clear and deep intuition, on the marvelous truth that in Christ Jesus the Lord we have life and stability. We do not become God, but we can become what pleases God. This relationship is a gift, not a reward, of God's own self.

Fourth, purity of heart, as I am describing it, means that I know God in my life as the true condition of my life. I may not know much else, but this I know (as said by the formerly blind man of John 9, who was healed by Jesus): "One thing I do know, that though I was blind, now I see" (John 9:25b). My true condition, the deepest reality in me, is that I do really love God and really want to be conformed to God's image. To live with this aspiration as the determining factor in my attitudes and behaviors is to have purity of heart. It is, as some have said, "to will one thing." That one thing, through all my personal triumphs and failures, is God's will.

So, is purity of heart a possibility for you? Yes, it is. But you will never attain purity of heart if you keep your eyes focused on yourself. Our lives are too complicated and too conflicted to give us much hope for success. Only the hopeless megalomaniac really believes in personal purity apart from God. But if you keep your spiritual eyes focused on the Lord, God will make you exactly what you should be as a child of grace. A writer I read for my own spiritual growth says our purity will probably be hidden from others, maybe even from ourselves. Actually, we are known fully only by God. The great selfless saints have consistently thought themselves to be full of sin. I think closeness to God brings out the realization in us of how far we are from God, and that we can be close to God only through God's grace. I have found that desiring to be close to God does not make one "holier than thou" (Isaiah 65:5, King James Version), or full of pride. No, quite the reverse. Closeness to God, or the desire to be close to God, fills one's life with humility and gratitude.

Holiness of life (purity of heart or, in a more traditional language, Christian perfection) is not for one's self alone. As we have seen in the preceding chapter, we exist not only for God but also for others. We delight in helping others. In the next chapter, we will see that the work of the Spirit in us blossoms in a fellowship of aspiring people. We call that fellowship "the church."

Concluding Thoughts

John Wesley strongly believed that purity of heart is a spiritual life entered by a decision and maintained by continuing decisions to constantly pursue this fullness of the Spirit. Many have taken issue with him at this point, but few have been willing to say he is totally wrong. Our most precious relationships are maintained by a series of commitments, each succeeding the other in intensity. Anyone who has spent a lifetime in a particular career knows that advancement did not happen by accident. Along the way were renewed pledges or promises to stick it out in spite of momentary pressures, disappointments, or temptations to move elsewhere. We probably choose our spouse many times in a marriage, because there are always tests to a relationship and strains with which one has to deal. Our spiritual lives are jump-started again and again as we face temptations, puzzling problems, and boredom. John Wesley believed that purity of heart is a chosen quest, begun deliberately and kept up deliberately.

Wesley calls you and me to a high goal, which is admittedly too high for many to even consider. This goal is tested in our time when concerned parents have to guard their children against child molesters and sellers of pornography who are on the Internet. The common morality of our movies and television programs, of our understandings of human origins and social interaction, is based more on a sort of intuitive sense of right and wrong rather than on the expectations of a moral, totally loving, and just God. The standard for many is in the mirror rather than in the Bible. Wesley calls us to choose against the tide and to commit to the highest in love and self-giving. To what end do we do this? To the glory of God, the one we love with all we are and know as the only reliable basis for our relationships with others, our only hope for personal and global peace.

To end this chapter is to do more than merely sum up our findings or take a theological position on an issue; it is to say yes to God in a new way. This is not to say you have not said yes to God before, even many times. Actually, this is a bit difficult to describe. Perhaps we should hear Wesley firsthand and let him direct us. In the conclusion of his sermon "On Sin in Believers," Wesley speaks to the spiritual sensitivity of those who want in every way possible to please God. Paraphrasing Wesley's thoughts, we hear:

> Let us hold fast the sound teaching given to our ancestors and handed down from generation to generation to us: Although we have been renewed and made inwardly clean by our faith in Christ, we are well aware that we still struggle against our own humanity, our tendency to make wrong choices, to listen to the wrong voices. Friends, let us be diligent, as the apostle says, to "[fight] the good fight of faith." Let us be earnest in prayer so that our inward sinfulness will not get the best of us. Rather, let us "put on the whole armor of God" and fight against anything that would drag us down. Let us resist what is bad so that we might be able to withstand the evil around us and, having done all we can, stand firm in God.[8]

Fortunately, we do not have to "[fight] the good fight" alone. The Holy Spirit strengthens us, and a supporting fellowship of believers helps us. It is to them that we now turn in our search for Wesleyan spirituality.

Probing Our Faith

1. Read carefully the Sermon on the Mount (Matthew 5–7) and the Sermon on the Plain (Luke 6:17-49). Try to grasp the entirety of Jesus' teaching and its meaning within your relationships.

2. Think about the things that attract and repel you. Write on a sheet of paper your goals in life and the priorities you set for yourself. What comes first, and why; what comes second; and so forth. John Wesley wants to help us realize that when we look at ourselves, we often see competing loyalties tugging at us.

3. John Wesley continually preached against works-righteousness, that is, the idea that eternal life is a reward for being good. If we could be rewarded for our good works, then the cross of Christ would be of no significance. Why would that be true?

4. As far as you know, what is the true condition of your life before God? On what do you base your answer?

ENDNOTES

1 From "The Character of a Methodist," in *The Works of John Wesley*, Volume VIII (Grand Rapids: Zondervan Publishing House, 1872 reprint), page 341.

2 See "A Plain Account of Christian Perfection," in *The Works of John Wesley*, Volume XI (Grand Rapids: Zondervan Publishing House, 1872 reprint), page 401.

3 From "The Circumcision of the Heart," in *The Works of John Wesley*, Volume 1, edited by Albert C. Outler, pages 413–14. © 1984 Abingdon Press. Used by permission. Footnote 128 at the bottom of page 413 states that Outler thinks these quotations are from "older devotional texts known to Wesley and to at least some of his audience."

4 From "The Great Privilege of Those That are Born of God," in *The Works of John Wesley*, Volume 1, edited by Albert C. Outler, page 439. © 1984 Abingdon Press. Used by permission.

5 From "Groaning for Full Redemption," in *The Works of John Wesley*, Volume 7, edited by Franz Hildebrandt and Oliver A. Beckerlegge, with the assistance of James Dale, page 503. © 1983 Abingdon Press. Used by permission.

6 From *The Unpublished Poetry of Charles Wesley: Hymns and Poems on Holy Scripture*, Volume II, edited by S. T. Kimbrough, Jr., and Oliver A. Beckerlegge, pages 23–24. © 1990 Abingdon Press. Used by permission.

7 From "A Single Intention," in *The Works of John Wesley*, Volume 4, edited by Albert C. Outler, page 377. © 1987 Abingdon Press. Used by permission.

8 From "On Sin in Believers," in *The Works of John Wesley*, Volume 1, edited by Albert C. Outler, pages 332–34. © 1984 Abingdon Press. Used by permission.

Chapter 6

The Spirit and the Church

*W*hen we sit at our computers peering at a seventeen-inch screen, we are not much different than our ancestors who once stared at images they painted on the sides of their caves. Their images and our computers attempt the same thing: to control the unknown and assure some kind of immortality. A painted animal may have been hope for success on the hunt or a magical way to provide protection against the danger the beast portrayed. Like our distant relatives, we fight imaginary battles with horrible foes on our video games, and thus control the forces of evil to the same extent they did, at least in our imaginations. We can visit a virtual cemetery on the Web that promises our loved ones will be remembered forever if we enshrine their names there. That is not much different than placing bowls of food, knives, and a change of clothes in prehistoric graves.

From the earliest times, we humans have tried to manage reality, in an attempt to guarantee a sense of well-being, to stave off the threats of the lawless, and to deliver us from the greatest fear of all: death. As in primeval days, we continue to build communities for protection. Once there were villages; now there are cities. Once there were spears and clubs of fire; now there are weapons capable of staggering destruction. In whatever age and by whatever means, humans try to understand their world and soften its dangers. This is a basic need that the gospel addresses.

The fact that we have some sense of being alive, of togetherness, of what it means to do wrong and do right, of family values is what makes us human. Even when such senses are warped or brutalized, we still have a faint hope that things can be better. This has forced us to live with ambiguity. We see that confusion in national leaders who have been despots, maniacs bent on destruction. On the other hand, some leaders have been humanitarians seeking the public good. Some artists have presented a terrifying view of the world, others a romantic, idealized view. Some parents are little more than tyrants; others are self-giving and authentically loving. By the same token, some communities are tainted, greedy, and fearful; others, however, are creative, helpful, and secure. History tells us that the same thing is true of church leaders and church groups. Some have attempted to control and manipulate; others have set our spirit free. In this ambiguity we live and try to listen to Christ through his church.

John and Charles Wesley had a grand view of the church. To them, the church of Jesus Christ is a divine reality, a series of symbols depicting a view of God's free grace and human free will. The church is an incubator wherein newborn people can grow in security, mature in their faith, and become holy in their aspirations to serve. The Wesleys had a beautiful view of Christianity as wholesome, patient, and strong. Christianity is God's alternative to the shattered communities of ordinary human life. No doubt the church as we know it has many problems; yet Wesley kept looking for that church Jesus described when the Lord told Peter that on the "rock" (of Peter's confession?) Christ would build the church (Matthew 16:18). Wesley also knew that we cannot go it alone, that humans need others to grow, and that the highest virtues require saintly models. The rugged individualism typified in the I-gotta-be-me idea will not work. It takes a church to raise a child of God. It takes the family of God.

In this chapter, we will see how the church, as the community of faith and worship, nurtures and shapes that life so that it is acceptable to God. This church is more than an institution; for the Wesleys, it was the collective spirit of those born of God, led and nurtured by the Holy Spirit of God. The Wesleys' view of the church will lead us finally to the hope of heaven, what John Wesley calls "the kingdom of glory,"[1] the crowning reality to the holy life. We will study that kingdom in the next chapter.

The Eternal Optimist

Nothing is served by sticking our heads in the sand in the face of the sins of the church. Again and again the prophets thundered against a wayward people. Jesus warned against infidelity, and Paul and Jude had some harsh things to say about those who abused the good name of God and the reputation of the church of God. The problem of sin for the church is precisely in that the people of the church, as the called-out people of God, are expected to have higher values than those around them, to be more self-giving than the average person, and to have hope in precisely those circumstances where others cave in. So when a revered preacher wallows in sexual infidelity, when a clergyperson embezzles some of the church's money, or when laypeople are caught in the abuse of power, the whole church reels under the exposure and criticism. I have known young ministers who left the church because they were disillusioned by betrayal and backbiting within the ranks of the faithful (or, better perhaps, the *unfaithful*).

Yet such examples of sin are not the church—not really. We need to look to those people who are loving, self-sacrificing, and loyal to get a real example of Christ's saving grace at work. The Wesleys agreed with this. They saw many bad apples in the church's barrel. Nonetheless, the church—the true church—is an act of God in the midst of the people. The church is a creation of grace, a place where humans can rise above themselves by the steadfast love of God. Because the Wesleys always kept in view the power of God to change human life for the better and to keep changing life for the better through all time, they were eternal optimists.

Charles Wesley characterizes the first-century church as a "mystic fellowship of love." In his hymn "Primitive Christianity, Part I," he says of the faithful:

Meek, simple followers of the Lamb,
They lived, and spake, and thought the same,
They joyfully conspired to raise
Their ceaseless sacrifice of praise.

With grace abundantly endued,
A pure, believing multitude,
They all were of one heart and soul,
And only love inspired the whole.[2]

Here we have clearly stated Charles Wesley's (and John's) notion that the true mark of the church is love. In "Primitive Christianity, Part II," Charles appeals to the "great builder" of the church:

The few that truly call thee Lord,
And wait thy sanctifying word,
And thee their utmost Saviour own,
Unite, and perfect them in one.[3]

Charles Wesley goes on to pray that God will "perfect holiness" in those who bow at God's feet. Wesley's hope is that such Christians will show others, especially critics, "how Christians lived in days of old." The primary example of this is seen in Christ, the "lowly Lord," who washes feet and serves others. At the end of this poetic description of faithful people, Wesley asks God to answer his prayer and be with the church forever:

Tell me, or thou shalt never go,
"Thy prayer is heard; it shall be so."
The word hath passed thy lips, and I
Shall with thy people live and die.[4]

And why should we not want to live and die with these people? They are the ones who, understanding their own needs, have looked to God for grace. In turn, they try to live out the will of the Lord in their private and public lives. Within this nurturing and growing body of people, we have the best chance for living a holy life. This people of this body reinforce our intention to do good and to be good. We can count on their prayers, their example, and their support. As we grow, we do the same for those following us. Thus grace never ends, and high aspirations are continually affirmed. We can feel ourselves surrounded and upheld by love. We are part of a people, the people who love God and want the best for others. This is a grand communion, one in which we are made and remade all the time and are forgiven.

Is this too much to hope for? Is such a community only a pipe dream? Apart from the grace of God, yes. With the grace of God, no. Such a community is different from those we already know. Many of us live and work in groups flawed to the point that we are distressed and think honesty and fair play is a joke. Yet God's grace always produces hope, and for us and the Wesleys, the real church of Christ (the one built upon the rock) is graced to rebound from its own failings, filled with spiritual energy to help us make it, and desirous only to please God in everything. Grinding out our daily lives is easier when we know that we are part of such a people.

Unity of Heart

The Christian doctrine of the Trinity is concerned with the unity of God. The Trinity is a great mystery, but it is a mystery in unity. This is to say that God is one, not many. We are taught about God in Scripture as Father, Son, and Holy Spirit. In one of his last-recorded prayers, our Lord prayed to God:

> The glory that you have given me I have given them, so that they may be one, as we are one. I in them and you in me, that they may become completely one, so that the world may know that you have sent me and have loved them even as you have loved me.
>
> (John 17:22-23)

Whatever else this passage means, it clearly means that Christians are one with God and one with each other. It also means that regardless of the wide variety we see in the universal church in terms of worship style, doctrinal emphasis, and church polity, the church is one. I am brother to those who are Baptist, Roman Catholic, Pentecostal, Russian Orthodox, and any other Christian grouping you can imagine. This is not a matter of whether they accept me as brother (which I am sure they do); I am one automatically by our collective commitment to Christ's teaching. This unity is a unity in love as a gift from God. This is so important that Jesus says that in some way the world's experience of God's saving grace is dependent on this unity (John 17:23). I cannot afford to be divisive or an isolationist. If I am, I bring shame on the good news, as well as on my brothers and sisters.

This alone, the notion that we believers are really members of the same family and should be eating at the same Communion Table, draws me to the Wesleys with appreciation and pride. John Wesley preached that the unity of the church is seen in four ways.

First, unity stems from humility, the desire to be a servant to others.

Second, unity stems from a willingness to endure hardship. When my sisters and brothers in another part of the world hurt, I hurt.

Third, unity stems from having patience. Paul said patience is a virtue; anyone who sits on a church board knows Paul is right. We can be patient because God is patient with us.

Fourth, unity stems from the active desire to keep relationships with other Christians strong and intact.

Clearly, the kind of real unity we have with one another comes from above. At one point in my ministry, the bishop sent me to a parish that had suffered a violent split. I was to serve that congregation until a permanent minister was appointed. As it turned out, I was with them for eighteen months. Christians, even close friends, were divided against one another. One group left the mother church and built its own church a few miles down the road. The two congregations began competing against each other, rather than working together for the upbuilding of the kingdom of God in that community. I tried to bridge the hurt feelings, the sense of betrayal, and the heavy judgment each group leveled at the other. I can say only that after I left, and after the effective ministry of the next two pastors, the deadening history of anger and resentment gradually healed. The basic problem was easy to see: Many of the people (not all) took their eyes off of the humble Christ and looked at themselves and at a person passing himself off as a spiritual leader. Christians on both sides could talk about humility, enduring suffering for Christ, being patient, and working for unity; but they could not do it with one another. They could not do it because they chose not to do it. It was as simple as that. Instead of embracing each other with repentance, many hardened their positions and became defensive.

Christ does not ask us if we want to be related to one another any more than we asked to be born into the family in which we were. Holy living involves the hard work of adjusting and coping with one another in order to bring glory to Christ, and to show those around us that the alternative community of Christ is for real.

A Place of Nurture Through the Spirit of Grace

John Wesley did not start out to found a new denomination. That much seems clear. What Wesley did want to do was reform the existing church, that is, help bring it back to its apostolic roots and early zeal. The Christian cause is not necessarily helped by splintering off into branches and sects. The heart of the Wesleyan Renewal Movement was the desire to help people become fully formed in Christ. This is what Wesley means by being holy. Being holy is to have the mind of Christ, as we have seen. The institutional church plays a profound role in that kind of spiritual formation. You see, the spiritual church of the faithful is known only by the name of Christian, but institutional churches bear many labels. The invisible church helps the visible church. The invisible church inspires and brings spiritual life. The visible church provides form for worship and service. The United Methodist Church is a form, something like a shell, for the spiritual energy of the Holy Spirit and the people of God to fill. Obviously, The United Methodist Church is not the only form available, but it is one.

What makes the church a place of nurture, a place in which Christians are brought to full maturity in Christ? The answer is plain and clear: It is the Holy Spirit of God. And how does the Holy Spirit do the necessary work in us? For John Wesley, it was through the witness of the Spirit in us and to one another. The Wesleys were convinced that when the apostle Paul said to the Christians at Rome: "When we cry, 'Abba! Father!' it is that very Spirit bearing witness with our spirit that we are children of God"

(Romans 8:16), he meant what he said literally. We might say that the Spirit of God impresses on our hearts that we really belong to God, that we are accepted by God.

John Wesley wrote three sermons on this witness, two of them on the witness of the Holy Spirit and one on the witness of our own spirit. What is this divine witness? What does Wesley mean? He means that God confirms to us in a way we can realize that our sins have been forgiven and that we live in the new life provided by Jesus Christ the Lord. Wesley points out that this is no new teaching but one found in Scripture and in the church's historic teaching. But try as he might, Wesley has difficulty helping us understand exactly what Paul means. In his sermon "The Witness of the Spirit, I," John Wesley says this "witness" is an "inward impression" that we are children of God. In saying this, Wesley moves us beyond the hope for eternal salvation to the realization of it in our experience.

The idea of knowing for sure that God is working in our life has been a problem for many people. When I first started preaching, someone suggested that I pass out small printed versions of the Gospel of John to anyone who came to me inquiring about God. These little booklets had in the front a special page, sort of a decision page that contained words something like this: "Today I have asked Christ to come into my heart and save me." The person could sign her or his name and date it on a line provided. The idea was that when that person was tempted to doubt God's working in her or his life, that person could reread the page and be reminded of that commitment. Now it was up to God to do God's part. The Wesleys mean something considerably different from this. We do not need small booklets with special pages. John Wesley says that God acts on our hearts by bringing a calm where there had been unrest, a sense of satisfaction that God has forgiven our sins.

How all this takes place is beyond Wesley and beyond me. Wesley would not argue over how it happens, but he wanted to show us that it can and does happen. But suppose I cannot honestly say I have such a witness from God—what then? No matter, John Wesley says; simply live in the faith that God is with you. God's witness will come in God's own time. We are not to wait, filled with dread or questions about the witness; rather, we are to live actively for God, and this inner confirmation will come when it pleases God.

Charles Wesley once wrote a wonderful prayer to the Holy Spirit that shows his continual desire to be led by and filled with the Spirit. The fourth of its six stanzas has special meaning.

> My peace, my life, my comfort thou,
>   My treasure and my all thou art!
> True witness of my sonship, now
>   Engraving pardon on my heart,
> Seal of my sins in Christ forgiven,
> Earnest of love, and pledge of heaven.[5]

The Spirit is addressed as divine, as indeed the church believes. The Spirit is described as Wesley's "peace," "life," "comfort," "treasure," "witness," "seal" (of pardon), and "earnest...pledge of heaven." How did Wesley arrive at such confidence? By his life of loving faith and the teaching of Scripture, Charles Wesley believed in God's grace and believed that it was given to him. Note the use of the word *engraving* (not just *engraved*), by which Wesley means that God is always at work. In the fifth stanza, Wesley prays: "With clearer light thy witness bear." This gracious man, filled with zeal for Christ, asked for clearer light. Because he was anxious? No. Because he was in love with God.

John Wesley's sermons on the witness of the Spirit were attempts by him to provide some objective ground for the assurance of salvation. Assurance has a subjective side, too, which we will now touch on briefly. Wesley begins his sermon "The Witness of Our Own Spirit" by saying that it will show "the nature and ground"[6] of Christian happiness. The question is, Can I know myself; can I know my own moods, my own commitments? If we are able to interact with others and with God, then we are able to say yes to that complex question. The joy of Christians is that in their hearts they can know and respond to the love of God with as much assurance as they are able to experience and express.

A subjective experience of that same assurance is based on the truthfulness of Scripture and the reliability of our normal capacity to respond to truth. I am not attempting to lay down some convincing argument to change someone's mind; neither is Wesley. But

Wesley is certainly saying that in the normal course of spiritual experience, our soul, heart, and mind sense the reality of God's grace active in our life, and we respond to that grace with joy. Furthermore, to keep the commandments—in particular Jesus' commandment to love one another—is a source of joy because we have found through experience that God is good and that God works for our good in what happens to us. The plain fact is that the Christian experience of God is fulfilling, helpful, and genuinely happy. At times we feel God intuitively and can no more doubt God's love than we can doubt our response to God.

Before leaving this subject, we need to listen to Luke. John Wesley's sermon "Scriptural Christianity" is based on a short segment from Acts 4:31. The context of that verse is a prayer meeting in which the first believers were together, asking God to make them bold in proclaiming Christ: "When they had prayed, the place in which they were gathered together was shaken; and they were all filled with the Holy Spirit and spoke the word of God with boldness." The central words from this great verse for Wesley are "and they were all filled with the Holy Spirit." Wesley says that in this wonderful outpouring of the Spirit, the "fruit" of the Spirit was given to the people gathered there in Christ's name. This word *fruit* comes from Paul's Letter to the Galatians (5:22): "The fruit of the Spirit is love, joy, peace, patience, kindness, generosity, faithfulness, gentleness, and self-control." Look at that list. The Spirit produces these attitudes in the lives of those who want and strive to please God. (Some people just require a little longer than others.) These attitudes and resulting behaviors come from the Spirit and are themselves evidence of the Spirit at work. Given the hostile environment in which the first Christians lived, absolutely without question this fruit came from God.

The first fruit on the list is love, for love paves the way for the rest of the fruit. Look at a Christian and ask yourself: *Do I see love at work? Do I see a person happy with God? Does this person have peace in believing? Is this person in some way patient, kind, and generous? Is faithfulness alive in this person? And gentleness and self-control—is this fruit apparent in this person to some degree?* Now look in the mirror and ask these same questions of

the one you see there. Wesley says this fruit is blooming in those
who live to do good to others in whatever ways they can, such as
visiting the sick, the prisoners, and the poor. Such people are the
"light of the world," set by God on a hill so that their light shines
to all around (Matthew 5:14-16). Such reactions of the Christian to
God's action become the norm, not the exception. I am not describing a person whose life displays no contradictions, no occasional
doubts, no personality problems. Neither is Wesley describing a
person who must force her or himself to be happy, or to appear
that way. Christians are real people (problems and all), and their
faith is real. But room for improvement is always apparent.

This attitude comes from the "mind" of Christ, which the Holy
Spirit is "engraving" in us. Sometimes we love by overlooking the
faults of our brother or sister in the faith; our patience shows in
our attitude of forgiveness; and our self-control keeps us from
doing or saying what may embarrass us or others. God has created
us as human beings, and we grow as human beings. Our delight is
that in many ways—some more obvious than others—God is making in the "kingdom of grace" a new people fit for the "kingdom
of glory."[7] Actually, the more we know about ourselves, the more
we can see God helping us overcome the problems we have. We
learn to say with Paul:

> It is no longer I who live, but it is Christ who lives in me. And the
> life I now live in the flesh I live by faith in the Son of God, who
> loved me and gave himself for me.   (Galatians 2:20)

Concluding Thoughts

John Wesley was no systematic theologian or philosopher. He
was not interested in splitting hairs over religious definitions. John
Wesley was much more interested in how God relates to human
beings in the concrete affairs of life. This is why Wesley's view of the
church lacks precision and is filled with generalities. John Wesley did
not want to spend time trying to work out nice and neat categories
of religious thought. He was too practical and, like ancient Israel,
concentrated instead on God's steadfast love and reliability. When
John Wesley looked at the church, he did not think, *Well, a good*

church is impossible. Rather, he thought, *God is faithful and will bring the church to its fruition through this life and into the next.* For both Wesleys, the greatness of God is in God's relatedness to us, not in some abstract formula, however intellectually stimulating. This is to say, God acts. And God acts in "witnessing" (or impressing on us) that God is working on our behalf.

The church is the community of faithful ones who worship and serve the faithful God. What does this mean for us? It means that we should always keep our eyes on God, as expressed in the incredible life and ministry of Jesus. Forget about useless speculation on ideas that have no practical value. Do not quibble about a definition of holiness, for it is better to pray and work for holiness. Avoid trying to defend your Christian faith; simply live deeply your new life in Christ. Listen to God's Holy Spirit.

Keep an eye open to God's future. It is to that future that we will turn in the next chapter.

Probing Our Faith

1. Think of the church you attend. Make a list of the ways you see God at work in the life of your congregation. How can God use you to help your church fulfill its ministry? Remember, fulfilling the church's ministry is never merely a matter of age or talents.
2. Think of your own religious history. With how many churches have you been associated? In what ways is your present church different from churches you have known in the past? In what ways is your church like them? Does what you find have meaning for you?
3. Do you have hurts that remain from your association with Christian people? If so, take time now to pray for those people. What would Christ have you do about those hurts?
4. To what extent are you convinced that God is your Redeemer, and that God is working on your behalf? What do you think of John Wesley's view of the witness of the Spirit? Why do you answer as you do?

ENDNOTES

1 From "A Plain Account of Christian Perfection," in *The Works of John Wesley*, Volume 2, edited by Albert C. Outler, pages 107–8. © 1985 Abingdon Press. Used by permission.

2 From "Describing the Pleasantness of Religion," in *The Works of John Wesley*, Volume 7, edited by Franz Hildebrandt and Oliver A. Beckerlegge, with the assistance of James Dale, pages 98–99. © 1983 Abingdon Press. Used by permission.

3 From "Describing the Pleasantness of Religion," in *The Works of John Wesley*, Volume 7, edited by Franz Hildebrandt and Oliver A. Beckerlegge, with the assistance of James Dale, pages 100–1. © 1983 Abingdon Press. Used by permission.

4 From "Describing the Pleasantness of Religion," in *The Works of John Wesley*, Volume 7, edited by Franz Hildebrandt and Oliver A. Beckerlegge, with the assistance of James Dale, page 102. © 1983 Abingdon Press. Used by permission.

5 From "Groaning for Full Redemption," in *The Works of John Wesley*, Volume 7, edited by Franz Hildebrandt and Oliver A. Beckerlegge, with the assistance of James Dale, pages 532–33. © 1983 Abingdon Press. Used by permission.

6 From "The Witness of Our Own Spirit," in *The Works of John Wesley*, Volume 1, edited by Albert C. Outler, page 300. © 1984 Abingdon Press. Used by permission.

7 From "Upon Our Lord's Sermon on the Mount, VI," in *The Works of John Wesley*, Volume 1, edited by Albert C. Outler, page 582. © 1984 Abingdon Press. Used by permission.

Chapter 7

Living Today for God's Tomorrow

𝒯he cover sheet on my student's work read:

Second Sermon Manuscript
"The Kingdom Is Here!
Are You Ready?"
Dr. Mercer
PR610

At first I chuckled; then I circled the words *"The Kingdom Is Here! Are You Ready?" Dr. Mercer* and wrote in the margin "I hope so." But the more I thought about it, the more personal that question became. The text for the sermon was Luke 17:20-37. In it we read that Jesus' cross is looming larger; the end is near. Some religious leaders are questioning Jesus about the coming of the Kingdom. In his answer, the Lord tells them the Kingdom is in their midst—that is, the Kingdom is right there among them. Obviously, they cannot see that. The scene shifts. Jesus talks with his disciples, telling them about the Kingdom to come. What we have is a text that speaks both of a kingdom present and a kingdom future; hence, the title of my student's sermon. The statement "The Kingdom is here!" speaks of Jesus' presence among us. The question "Are you ready?" asks if we are anticipating God's future for us. Jesus' presence has two dimensions.

These two truths, the kingdom present and the kingdom future, were important to the Wesleys. The movement of history has a beginning and an end. John Wesley believed that human time is part of God's time, that is, eternity. The Bible speaks of God before creation and of God after the Final Judgment. Part of the Christian hope is that our history will give way to God's eternity, and that we will live forever with the Lord. Actually, we now live in two worlds (or two times) and have one foot in each of these worlds. We are citizens of two realms; the greater in terms of majesty and longevity is God's realm. My student's question is one the New Testament witnesses ask over and over again: Are you ready for God's coming kingdom?

The concerns of this chapter are the logical end of our probing on holy living. We will look closely at the Wesleys' hope of salvation in God's future for us. We will discover that holy living not only has a beginning, but it also has an end in view. In fact, the end for which we hope partially determines how we live our lives now. The conclusion following this chapter will remark on the broad sweep of our living out the gospel of our Lord Jesus Christ.

The Heaven of Love

We must not discount as sentimentalism the sense of happiness found in early Methodist singing. For example, in the section on "Describing the Pleasantness of Religion," in Charles Wesley's *Hymns,* we find these words:

> All fullness of peace, All fullness of joy,
> And spiritual bliss That never shall cloy;
> To us it is given In Jesus to know
> A kingdom of heaven, A Heaven below.[1]

Today, we are cautious about speaking quickly of "fullness of peace," "fullness of joy," and "spiritual bliss." Jesus, according to this hymn, is the source for us of "a kingdom of heaven" in this life—that is, "a heaven below." This may sound like a little too much to people today, since we are sensitive to human failing, even among the best of us. This is why I think Charles wisely inserted the phrase "that never shall cloy." But what does that mean? (When was the last time you used the word *cloy* in a sentence?) To cloy is to have too much of a good thing, like eating candy to the point of getting sick. Wesley was saying that his description of religious experience in Christ is not to be thought of as corny, gushy, or melodramatic. This is not like the old silent films in which an actress had to exaggerate facial expressions and gestures to get her emotions across to the audience. Rather, Wesley was saying that on a deep level, way past feelings, a Christian believer can know a kind of security and peace, something like a port in a storm. In this, Wesley is much like those Old Testament prophets who spoke of restoration and happiness to a generation in chains.

This message was crucial, and it was liberating to the common people in Wesley's England. When you go down into the mines before sunup and do not come out again until after sundown, when you may have to give up your four-year-old child to become a chimney sweep because you cannot afford to feed him, and when your sport is to watch bears and dogs fight to the death, you need to hear a good word. And when you hear that your miserable life is important to none other than the God of the universe, that God loves you to the point of dying on a cross, and that this same God wants to free you from guilt and actually put some hope in your heart, then you will know what joy is.

They may have been rude in their manners, but for thousands of the poor in the British Isles of the eighteenth century, emotions bubbled over publicly at the singing and preaching of the Methodist preachers. You may have heard the phrase *shouting Methodists*. Well, that phrase was literally true. Methodists shouted because they believed that God was taking them out of their bondage to prejudice, ignorance, and powerlessness and setting them free as fully formed sons and daughters of the great God. It would have been impossible to convince some of those English scrub women that their faith was simply a hysterical, delusional reaction. God's grace was their life!

It is amazing to me that many people who say they are religious continue to be skeptical of happiness, as though fragile and flawed humans simply cannot be at peace. Some actually think that our best moments do little more than faintly approximate the hope that is laid up in heaven for us. But the solution is not a matter of denying one's problems and being deaf to the inner voices of negativism and self-blame; the solution is a matter of sensing in one's own heart the magnificent truth of Wesley's words:

> Our Jesus receiving, Our happiness prove,
> The joy of believing, The heaven of love.[2]

"Seek First the Kingdom"

A split second is the interval between a child continually asking, "Momma, are we there yet?" and that same person at retirement asking, "Where did all the time go?" Jesus said life is like a wispy cloud, like summer grass. That's how short life is. Yet, what is most required in growing spiritually is time. Months and years are necessary for a person to truly discover what it means to follow God and to be changed into that follower. Seeking is a lifelong quest; finding occurs, but it always opens new possibilities for seeking. The twin facts that what we seek is so far above us and that we have so little time to seek it is what makes for urgency. If we are going to be disciples of Jesus, we need to start now and make Jesus' agenda our agenda, not just on Sundays but every single day and every waking hour. We are in for the long haul when we want to be found "in Christ."

This section's title, "Seek First the Kingdom," is the title of the second sermon John Wesley preached in his long and illustrious career. The sermon is based on Matthew 6:33 and is a sequel to his first sermon, "Death and Deliverance." In these two sermons the young Anglican deacon set forth themes he would herald for the rest of his evangelistic ministry: the reality of death, the tendency of people to deny death, the power of God to deliver from the terror of death, the blessedness of the redeemed in heaven, and the necessity of getting started on following Christ now. John Wesley's ministry began with an eye opened to the future of his soul. As I have mentioned elsewhere, Wesley's view of the next life shaped his preaching about this one. That is not surprising, is it? A strong belief that judgment and God await us when we close our eyes in death will make a lot of difference in how we view what we are doing now. Likewise, if we give no thought to tomorrow, today has a greatly reduced value.

Is that true? If we do not believe in heaven or in the possibility of it, doesn't that make today all the more important? Won't people live today to the hilt? Won't we be caring and busy about doing good? Won't we really seek our neighbor's good if we see this life as all she or he will have? Not really, says Wesley. All we need to do is look around us and take stock of what we see. The human race seems hell-bent on being selfish, using others, making war, and grabbing lands and goods. This situation—this rush to assert oneself, to project one's needs above others, and to deny the marginalized because our own supposed needs really mask deep fears about life and death—would be comic if it were not so tragic. Nevertheless, human energy will find a target at which to aim. That target may be profit, influence, cheating the system, or even saintliness. We will aim at something because what we aim at defines who we really are in the depths of our very being. You are what you seek.

Echoing the gospel, the Wesleys want us to seek the kingdom of God. This is especially hard for Christians today because, like our pop culture, we want fast results in a short amount of time. The fast-food mentality has invaded educational theory, even in seminaries. I was asked recently to teach a one-week intensive course on spiritual life for doctoral students. I did it but told the students that the course could not accomplish its objectives. They were paying for dinner, but what they were getting was an early snack, whose nutritional value was questionable. However, these students wanted a snack because these intensive courses were designed to meet their "needs." But the gospel understands that our needs have to be thought of in the light of Jesus' fourth beatitude: "Blessed are those who hunger and thirst for righteousness, for they will be filled" (Matthew 5:6).

Hungering, thirsting, seeking, waiting, and *journeying* are all biblical words for what it means to be serious about our faith. They are not words for a quick fix. If Wesley had been using the New Revised Standard Version of the Bible, he would have read Matthew 6:33 ("But strive first for the kingdom of God and his righteousness, and all these things will be given to you as well") in this way: Seek, strive, and then find; seek, strive, and then find; seek...

The King of Terrors

"The king of terrors" is what the Book of Job (18:14) calls death. The kingdom of God, in its present and future manifestations, is all mixed up with death. To seek the Kingdom is to confront death. Giving birth is normally a tangle of pain and joy; so is seeking the kingdom of God. Most of us have the opportunity of living long enough to face the reality of our own mortality and our own immortality. The early Methodists used to sing about death. One of the shorter hymns in the section on "Describing Death" in Charles Wesley's *Hymns* opens for us the central question of our spirituality:

> Pass a few swiftly fleeting years,
>   And all that now in bodies live
> Shall quit, like me, the vale of tears,
>   Their righteous sentence to receive.
>
> But all, before they thence remove,
>   May mansions for themselves prepare
> In that eternal house above—
>   And, O my God, shall I be there?[3]

That short, penetrating hymn is not found in *The United Methodist Hymnal* we use today. When we sing about death today, we sing for the most part about "eternal life" (the title of the section in our hymnal). We affirm eternal life and its impact on our growing quest for holiness of life. But the sensitivities of modern Methodists probably would be shocked at the first stanza of Charles Wesley's six-stanza hymn on a Christian view of death, which begins this way:

> Ah, lovely appearance of death!
>   What sight upon earth is so fair?
> Not all the gay pageants that breathe
>   Can with a dead body compare.
> With solemn delight I survey
>   The corpse when the spirit is fled,
> In love with the beautiful clay,
>   And longing to lie in its stead.[4]

If we read the full text of that hymn, we would find a rather sharp analysis of reality and Christian faith. We die; that is the truth. But in Christ we will live, and that, too, is the truth. Charles Wesley, who wrote that hymn to sing as "victory" at the death of a young man in Cardiff, wants us to know that our striving after Christ will have a triumphant end. Only when we try to hide as best we can the coldness of death does our faith seem lame when facing death. A final reference to Wesley's funeral hymns will help us grasp the tenacious faith of our forebears.

> Let the world bewail their dead,
>   Fondly of their loss complain;
> Brother, friend, by Jesus freed,
>   Death to thee, to us, is gain;
> Thou art entered into joy:
>   Let the unbelievers mourn,
> We in songs our lives employ,
>   Till we all to God return.

As the last two lines above say, "We in songs our lives employ, till we all to God return." Return we will; that is the truth. No matter how rugged the way, how filled with cruel experience and disappointment, ours is a way of growing spirituality until the day we enter into the joy of the Lord in a full and unhindered way. Seek first the kingdom!

The Kingdom of Glory

Many hymns and gospel songs that are familiar to United Methodists contain some reference to heaven, from the stately "The God of Abraham Praise" to the folksy "When We All Get to Heaven." Over and over again we affirm our conviction that our lives have eternal worth. In the great Apostles' Creed, we state that we believe in "life everlasting." Yet I have known Methodists, even pastors, who have had their fingers crossed behind their backs at this point in the Creed. Why do we so easily assume that the last breath is the last of life? That assumption is easy to understand from the standpoint of a naturalist-humanist. But from a Christian? Easter was no mere holiday for the Wesleys; it was the crown of God's life lived for us in Jesus, and the hope of our lives lived for God in Jesus. Jesus Christ's resurrection is our future; Christ's current life is our hope.

One of the benchmark sermons for John Wesley's view of our life in Christ is "Salvation by Faith," which he first preached on June 11, 1738, at St. Mary's, Oxford. Contained in that sermon is a good, concise statement of faith. The basic elements of our faith, Wesley says, are (1) a personal commitment to Christ; (2) continuing confidence in "the merits" of Christ's life, death, and resurrection for our lives; (3) trust that through Christ our sins are really forgiven; and (4) drawing close to Christ as our life and hope.[6] Thus, for Methodists, Christ is the center of God's reaching out to us, and Christ is the center of our lives and our future. This is salvation, to be in Christ, as Paul puts it, redeemed from sin and living with the Savior. As we know, this faith means true life in this world and true life beyond this world. This is the good news.

This sermon of Wesley's is packed. Christ is the focal point. In Christ we are reconciled to God by faith (trust). The emphases in the following statement are Wesley's: Christ given for us and living in us. Therefore we *close with him* (a Puritan phrase meaning becoming close to Christ) and *cleave to him* (cling to him as to no other). The result of our trusting and clinging, out of which issues our life and works, is salvation. And our ultimate salvation is finally being in heaven with God, doing God's will, and praising God for ever and ever. Redemption begins where sin did (on earth), and redemption extends into that reality where sin is excluded (the kingdom of glory, as John Wesley called it). This whole process is based on God's work for us in Christ Jesus, our Redeemer and Lord.

What will heaven be like? Of that we have few clues. The sparse information we have is understood differently by Christian interpreters. Even John Wesley was at a loss for words on this subject. His commentary on the Book of Revelation, the last book in the New Testament, was not basically his own. He freely admitted that he understood little about the book, and so he borrowed heavily from a German Christian scholar named Johann Albrecht Bengel, who himself wrote two long commentaries—one in Latin and the other in German—on that most mysterious book. Wesley's studies of Revelation and other biblical books did convince him of several things, however.

First, heaven is first of all a present inward experience. The Wesleys were convinced that God touches our lives with forgiveness, happiness, and hope. This is a "real" change in us. In this sense, we know something of what heaven will be like, in that it will enlarge and fill our lives to capacity with the reality and love of God. When we experience joy, we are getting a foretaste of what God has in mind for our future. When we experience pain, we have hope that one day God will wipe away our tears. We must remember that hoping is much more than wishing.

Second, heaven in us now helps us adjust our lives to the shifting values of our culture. We have looked at this many times in this book. This is simply to say that God's grace in us helps us identify and handle the temptations and artificial goals that come our way. Because our world is not yet delivered from the impact of sin, we must listen to God in prayer and in Scripture. Our worship with other Christians, plus our experience at Holy Communion, reinforces our confidence in the gospel as our deliverance and our end.

Third, heaven is a living hope that energizes our quest for holiness of heart and life. We seek the highest standard for ourselves, no matter how far short we fall from achieving that standard. God puts virtue in our lives as we turn our lives over to God. *Heaven* is that eternal word that maintains that we could never get to heaven on our own; heaven is God's everlasting gift. Because that is true, we can relax and simply live in God's sight, knowing our attempts at faithfulness will be met by God's free grace. To be holy is to be dedicated wholly to God, to seek God in the midst of life until we are with God forever.

Fourth, heaven is the goal of the church. Our lives are not lived alone, especially not our Christian lives. What Wesley calls "an innumerable company"[7] that surrounds us is made up of the faithful who have gone on before us, the memory of whom provides us with courage and resolve until Christ comes. We are part of a whole; we are brother or sister to others. Whenever we enter the sanctuary, no matter its size or location, we enter into a new reality, past and present. That reality is that our celebration, our worship and adoration, is but the beginning of our relationship with the redeemed of all ages.

Fifth, heaven is an enduring relationship. Virtually everything we see or touch in this life has limits. Our solar system is itself a birthing and dying system, with new constellations being formed and old stars going out. The grand redwood tree that existed at the time of Christ will one day die. The oldest living mammal is but a fleeting thought in comparison with eternity. Comets, trees, and elephants have no understanding of their peculiar life cycle. That knowledge is left to humans, which is God's gift to us and helps us prepare for the unimaginable: eternal life. With the image of God in us, we are heir to that One who knows no days or years.

A Personal Word

I have for many years read and written on various aspects of Wesley's view of holiness of heart and life and have found it baffling and challenging at the same time. The thought of taking seriously Peter's admonition "as he who called you is holy, be holy yourselves in all your conduct" (1 Peter 1:15) has always attracted me. At the same time, my multiple starts and stops, my repeated failures, have often dulled my spirit. For a long time I did not realize that God was actually calling me to be fully human, not fully angelic, to be what God created me to be: a sincere follower of Jesus, always learning from Christ what it means to pray and be faithful. I have also learned that if I am always checking my progress, I am doomed to depression; but if I keep my eyes on the Lord, God will do in me what I cannot do for myself. One other thing I have learned is never to use myself as an example of holiness. That is an invitation to disaster.

My journey has taught me not to try to imitate the spirituality of someone else. My own life in Christ has been seriously shaped by John Wesley, Thomas Merton (a monk and spiritual writer), and Francis of Assisi. Others have influenced by quest, of course, but these are the main ones.

Another one, however, deserves special mention: My wife, Ruth, has taught me by example the meaning of unconditional love, with no thought of appreciation returned or recognition received. I will stop with that. Those who really know her know what I mean.

But my admiration for these people must not fool me into trying to be someone I cannot be. I can be only myself, with my own personal problems and joys. The same is true for you as well. I must cling to Christ and be open to him in "the way" he has given me. I must trust Christ above my failings and count him my highest joy. When I say "must" I do not mean tasteless obligation but rarest privilege. After all, I know full well that my only hope is in him who is Lord without rival.

I have little concern with how my life may appear to others. However, I am not free from others, because I have an obligation to them as my relatives and fellow human beings. I work and pray for their good, just as I do for my own. What I continue to discover is how new this life in Christ really is. I began my trek with Christ in 1955, though prior positive influences had touched me, thank God. I have been privileged to spend my adult life studying Scripture and theology and sharing my findings with others, and for that also I thank God. After all, moments of grand insight and the application of truth still burst in upon me with the force of a new discovery. Those insights may not be new to others, but God has allowed them to become my truths, too. And I now know instinctively that these new flashes of reality must be lived out deeply—that is, deep within my own spirit and in my relationships with others.

At first I was a Methodist because it was in that church that I came to an awareness of the love of God. But now, after study, comparison, and questioning, I am committed to John Wesley's broad understanding of the way of salvation. I appreciate it for its emphasis on God's free grace and human free and responsible will, for its focus on the uniqueness of Jesus, and for its call to give one's life to the pursuit of holiness in life and in service. As the old (and no-longer-used) camp meeting song says: "I'm bound to march in endless bliss and die a shouting [smiling?] Methodist."[8] But more than being Methodist, may God make us Christian, and enable us continually to live deeply our new life in Christ.

Probing Our Faith

1. Why, do you think, do people hesitate or refuse to become Christ's followers? What objections have you heard as to why some people do not want to become Christian? How have you handled those objections?
2. Study advertising on television or in magazines. To what do these advertisements appeal in us? What do they want us to become, and what values do they want us to hold?
3. What changes will be necessary for you if you are to close with Christ and cling to Christ?
4. What images of heaven do you have, and where do you think they came from? Do the Wesleys shed any new light on heaven for you?

ENDNOTES

1 From "Describing the Pleasantness of Religion," in *The Works of John Wesley*, Volume 7, edited by Franz Hildebrandt and Oliver A. Beckerlegge, with the assistance of James Dale, page 103. © 1983 Abingdon Press. Used by permission.

2 From "Describing the Pleasantness of Religion," in *The Works of John Wesley*, Volume 7, edited by Franz Hildebrandt and Oliver A. Beckerlegge, with the assistance of James Dale, page 103. © 1983 Abingdon Press. Used by permission.

3 From "Describing Death," in *The Works of John Wesley*, Volume 7, edited by Franz Hildebrandt and Oliver A. Beckerlegge, with the assistance of James Dale, pages 137–38. © 1983 Abingdon Press. Used by permission.

4 From "Describing Death," in *The Works of John Wesley*, Volume 7, edited by Franz Hildebrandt and Oliver A. Beckerlegge, with the assistance of James Dale, page 138. © 1983 Abingdon Press. Used by permission.

5 From "Describing Death," in *The Works of John Wesley*, Volume 7, edited by Franz Hildebrandt and Oliver A. Beckerlegge, with the assistance of James Dale, page 141. © 1983 Abingdon Press. Used by permission.

6 See "Salvation by Faith," in *The Works of John Wesley*, Volume 1, edited by Albert C. Outler (Nashville: Abingdon Press, 1984), page 121.

7 From "Upon Our Lord's Sermon on the Mount, XI," in The Works of John Wesley, Volume 1, edited by Albert C. Outler, page 673. © 1984 Abingdon Press. Used by permission.

8 From "The Methodist," in *The Frontier Camp Meeting: Religion's Harvest Time*, by Charles A. Johnson (Dallas: Southern Methodist University Press, 1955), page 204.

Conclusion

Stair-Stepping

I have a standing luncheon on Saturdays with a friend who is an engineer and an author. Our conversations are predictable. We will at some time get around to theology, writing, and Kentucky basketball. The order in which we discuss these subjects varies according to the season. Recently, I asked Ben what spiritual goals he had set for himself. He knew at the time that I was preparing this book, and that my question stemmed from my research of the writings of the Wesley brothers. Our conversation was thick and fast. Ben got so excited that he splashed cocktail sauce on his shirt sleeve. Mixing a fair amount of philosophy, history, and spiritual writing together, we came up with two differing but often equally appealing ways to understand Christian life. We agreed to use the idea of climbing a staircase to illustrate what we were talking about. It is a different metaphor than that of the ocean, with which I started this book.

The first view represents those thinkers who look at life, even Christian life, as ascending a staircase that has increasing distance between steps. For example, the distance one might have to step up between the first and second step would be, say, eight inches; between the second and third, nine inches; and so forth. As you can see, the higher one climbs the stairs, the bigger the steps one must take to get to the next level. This represents those people who look at Christian life as a series of more and more difficult choices and greater and greater demands. For the spiritual life, this would mean increasing struggle as one seeks to draw nearer to God and grow more holy in heart and life. This illustration suggests that difficulties grow in intensity the more one seeks to please God. As a mutual friend of ours said about the idea of holiness of life, "Who wants it? Who wants to pay the price of sacrifice it requires to love God completely, to give up what one must give up?" In other words, a hesitation (perhaps a fear) lies deep in the heart of the true Christian about this business of being totally dedicated to God and holding nothing back. It looks like such a chore.

The second view represents those who look at life, even Christian life, as moving up a stair that has decreasing distance between steps. The larger steps would be at the beginning of the Christian life; the smaller steps would be later in one's spiritual development. The higher one goes, the easier it is to step from one level to another. From this perspective, Christian life is a series of increasing demands, but they are easier to accept. For the spiritual life, this would mean increasing ease as one seeks to draw nearer to God and to grow more holy in heart and life. This illustration suggests that openness to God grows the closer one wants to draw near to God. Instead of increasing struggle in our quest for God, the intensity of the struggle decreases over time and eventually ceases altogether. While there may well be early hesitations as more and more of the Christian life opens up to us and we see the severity of the adjustments we must make to be fully loving, those hesitations significantly lessen the more love comes to control the choices we make.

The second of these options for stair-stepping describes the optimism of the Wesley brothers and the way they understood how we grow in God. For the Wesleys, the more attention we give to our spiritual growth, the faster we grow and the easier it becomes. The central reason for this is that the more we experience God's love, the happier we become and the more of God we want. The more we want the will of God, the more appealing God's will becomes because God's will makes our lives complete and helps us become the best possible people we can be in this life. For the Wesleys, Christian life is not a wrestling match as much as it is a comfortable walk through life with a fully compatible companion. You see, the first giant step we take is the decision to follow Christ in the first place. According to John Wesley, that is when we move from being wholly self-absorbed people to being people freely open to God's choices and God's directions. Now we walk with God in a mutually loving relationship that spills over into all the other relationships we will ever have.

This understanding of Christian experience is truly freeing. God has not come into your life to make you miserable; God has come into your life to make you happy. This is what Wesley says, as we have seen. Without God our lives are miserable enough. We jump from interest to interest and from sin to sin in a vain attempt to have a meaningful life. What we cannot control we deny. Reality is hard to face, especially our own.

Sociologist Ernest Becker says most of us simply cannot face the fact that we will die. Therefore, we deny death by focusing our attention on more immediate matters, such as our jobs, our hobbies, our families, or anything else that will divert us from facing squarely that we—like every other living thing—will lay down and die. In fact, we are so afraid of death that we try to control it by joking about it or by going to war, and in that way assume the godlike ability to decide who lives and who dies. Becker is on target. This is the reason why many people get emotionally stuck at an adolescent level and do not want to assume adult responsibilities and adult decisions. Even in Las Vegas, an adult version of Disney World, losing is soothed with star-studded shows, exploding multicolored lights, and hotels designed as fantasy palaces.

God has come to us to make life meaningful and death more meaningful. The gift of eternal life as the consequence of faithfully following Jesus puts a whole new cast on why and how we live. The call to walk with God and become more like God in love, compassion, and service is a call to holiness because God is holy. To belong to God and reflect God's glory is the highest destiny of humankind. Desiring to be holy in thought and deed is strange only to those who are still wrapped up in themselves, who see life as somehow catering to their needs, who want to live life on their own terms and experience gratification now.

The theme of "reversal" is a main theme of the Gospels. It is seen in Mary's song in Luke's gospel, where we hear her saying:

> [God] has brought down the
>   powerful from their thrones,
>   and lifted up the lowly;
> he has filled the hungry with
>   good things,
>   and sent the rich away empty.
>   (Luke 1:52-53)

Mary's song shows a God who loves to turn the tables on those trying to take advantage of their power and make others miserable, or those who flaunt their wealth and do not share it with those in need. The order of life for the powerful and the rich seems to be the order of ordinary life. This was the dilemma of the writer of Psalm 73. He looked around and saw the jet set of his time; they had everything and he had nothing—at least that is how he tells it. He went so far as to say that he had followed God for nothing! The best thing to do is get off of this dead-end road and get with it. He was miserable. Then he went to worship. We are not told exactly what happened; but when the psalmist left the Temple, he could see clearly how wrong he had been. God had given him a glimpse of the larger picture, so that when he walked out of the Temple doors, he walked out a renewed man who wanted with all his heart to embrace the Lord God of Israel and live according to God's teachings. This is a reversal of the status quo. God is constantly coming to us, urging us to think about what God is saying and then to weigh it against what we see in a shortsighted, self-serving society.

For us to seek to be a holy people is a reversal of the values by which most people live. Even our desire to be a fully loving and giving people is at times seen as a guise for selfishness and a desire to manipulate. I certainly admit that holiness can be faked and that love can be twisted into perversion. At the same time, many—yes, very many—people all over the world want with all their hearts to please the living God and live lives that demonstrate that desire. Until I began to study seriously the religious consciousness of Christian groups the world over, I never realized the vast numbers of people who want love more than influence, compassion more than power, and goodness more than selfishness. That study has revitalized my confidence in Wesley's notion of Christian perfection in love as an important ideal for Christian striving. What must change in us at the outset, however, is a turning away from the open cynicism, which characterizes much public judgment on goodness and mercy, and turn to the teachings of Jesus and the power of the Spirit. It is past time that we own again this vision of Peter:

> You are a chosen race, a royal priesthood, a holy nation, God's own people, in order that you may proclaim the mighty acts of him who called you out of darkness into his marvelous light.
>   Once you were not a people,
>   but now you are God's people;
>   once you had not received mercy,
>   but now you have received mercy.   (1 Peter 2:9-10)

I strongly urge you, my reader, my friend, to take the Wesleyan message of true life to heart, to struggle with its meaning, and to enjoy something of the freedom it proposes. Open your heart to the fresh wind of the Spirit of God, to the continuing new life Christ brings to you. Realize yourself on the road to heaven, with stops to help others along the way. And may the great God who has called you to the kingdom of glory fill you with love, kindness, patience, and joy in your journey from the tide pool to the heavy-breathing ocean of our new life in Christ.